D1446205

SUPERVISION IN EDUCATION

A Differentiated Approach with Legal Perspectives

Bernadette Marczely, EdD, JD

Professor
College of Education
Cleveland State University
Cleveland, Ohio

AN ASPEN PUBLICATION
Aspen Publishers, Inc.
Gaithersburg, MD
2001

Library of Congress Cataloging-in-Publication Data

Marczely, Bernadette.
Supervision in education : a differentiated approach with legal perspectives /
Bernadette Marczely.
p. cm.
Includes bibliographical references and index.
ISBN 0-8342-1856-9
1. School supervision—United States 2. Teacher effectiveness—United States. 3.
Teachers—Rating of—United States. I. Title.

LB2806.4 .M37 2000
371.2'01—dc21
00-041609

Orders: (800) 638-8437
Customer Service: (800) 234-1660

About Aspen Publishers • For more than 40 years, Aspen has been a leading professional publisher in a variety of disciplines. Aspen's vast information resources are
available in both print and electronic formats. We are committed to providing the
highest quality information available in the most appropriate format for our cus-
tomers. Visit Aspen's Internet site for more information resources, directories, articles,
and a searchable version of Aspen's full catalog, including the most recent publications: **www.aspenpublishers.com**
Aspen Publishers, Inc. • The hallmark of quality in publishing
Member of the worldwide Wolters Kluwer group.

Editorial Services: Ruth Bloom
Library of Congress Catalog Card Number: 00-041609
ISBN: 0-8342-1856-9
Printed in the United States of America
1   2   3   4   5

I would like to thank my husband David for his technical and moral support in helping me to complete this project.

—*Bernadette Marczely*

Table of Contents

Introduction: Overcoming Legal and Contractual Obstacles

rofessional accountability has become the slogan for every plan
to reform public education. However, professional accountability, like every other aspect of reform in public education,
has been painted with broad and sweeping strokes, describing very
generalized expectations. There is an assumption that one singular
set of procedures, a rubric for summative evaluation, exists to ensure
professional accountability in all circumstances. Present accountability systems ignore the fact that teachers are at different stages in
career development and that what an entry-level teacher can and
should be held accountable for may be quite different from what is
expected of a midcareer or veteran teacher. Present accountability
systems also tend to ignore or downplay the role of the school district in remediating recognized problems.

The idea of personalizing professional accountability and differentiating supervision is at odds with the way teachers are presently
supervised and evaluated, and the so-called reformers seem unable
to get beyond traditional expectations and approaches. Their inertia
is reinforced by the influence that collective bargaining has had on
the quest for professional accountability. Collectively bargained
evaluation procedures standardize rather than individualize. Varia-
tions in practice may develop good instruction, but they are viewed
as an anathema to those looking for comparable information to use
in making assessments.[1] Collectively bargained contracts more often

than not dictate the form and substance of teacher accountability, and, by virtue of the contract, all teachers are treated alike in matters of formal supervision and accountability. The contract may determine whether a preconference is needed, dictate the format and focus for any observations required, and define the time lines and ultimate effect of the supervision, evaluation and mandated observations and postconferences.

Even when accountability prescriptions are not set by contract, district lawyers may advise administrators to use one common approach in evaluating teachers in order to avoid claims of discrimination and harassment. Fear of litigation, not fear of failure, drives present methods for assessing professional accountability. This fear of litigation has had a definite hand in taking *individual* considerations out of the accountability formula. In short, there is little room for guesswork or concern for individuality in the professional accountability and supervision processes as they now exist, and administrators who vary from negotiated or legally prescribed procedures know that they do so at their own risk.

This effort to ensure accountability by prescription is robed in the mantle of equity and fairness; however, it is ultimately unfair to teachers and students, and responsible for the perceived ineffectiveness of teacher evaluation and the inequity in performance found in the classroom. Evaluation and supervision, as they are presently conducted, are perceived as empty rubric by administrators, teachers, and the public at large. After all is said and done, how good can supervision and an accountability plan be if students continue to perform below accepted norms on proficiency tests and national assessments? What are teachers to be held accountable for, if not their individual role in the ongoing progress and ultimate performance of their students? Accountability plans that ignore individuality sacrifice progress and performance to a false perception of equity and efficiency.

Growing numbers of highly competent teachers are frustrated by present evaluation practice.[2,3] For their part, administrators see teacher evaluation as a routine checklist activity undertaken to fulfill bureaucratic requirements, rather than to inform individual or institutional improvement efforts.[4] Typically, supervisors complete rating checklists and write evaluative reports of teacher performance without teachers having an opportunity to confer about observations or the evaluative criteria used. Thus, neither teachers nor administrators see the process as having any real or lasting effect on personal professional missions or fates. The process has been reduced to an exercise of form, not substance.

External means of enforcing accountability, such as state proficiency tests, evoke far more trepidation and personal response than do most district evaluation plans. Proficiency testing, after all, has the potential to hold individual schools, principals, and teachers responsible for the performance of their students in a very public and irrefutable way. Teacher performance assessment has become an inherent part of proficiency testing accountability. School boards and parents can now identify the child, the school, and the teachers, and can link their performances through proficiency test reporting.

Proficiency accountability, however, is one-dimensional. It is used to unmask failure or deficiencies, but it does nothing to address professional accountability for average or above-average performing students and teachers. Proficiency testing sets minimal standards for teacher and student performance. Thus, the question must be posed as to whether this bar of minimum performance should continue to be the sole effective means to measure professional accountability. If, indeed, it is, there will be little incentive to strive for achievement beyond the basics tested. Unless other avenues of supervision are adopted as well, the pursuit of excellence will be replaced by the maintenance of mediocrity.

Taking the pursuit of excellence out of the accountability equation is a mistake of historic proportions. Yet, to dismiss the concept of individualized professional accountability is to do just that. It is the premise of this text that only accountability and supervision plans that focus attention on individual strengths, as well as weaknesses, and the professional needs of individual teachers will be effective in taking public education beyond basic achievement. The anonymity found in uniform evaluation plans makes it too easy to settle for the mediocre goals of group assessment. Anonymity inevitably destroys true accountability because it allows the individual to settle for group response. True professional accountability in education begins and ends with individual teachers responding effectively to the unique situations in which they find themselves at various times in their careers. Schools will never be more effective than the individual teachers in them, so attention to individual professional performance and goals becomes paramount to making schools as effective as they can be.

The problems that individual teachers encounter are closely tied to their professional maturity. In established professions, licensing tests are based on the body of knowledge that practitioners have decided newcomers must have. However, in teaching, that had not been the case until October 1999 when the Educational Testing Service announced a revamp of the tests in its PRAXIS Series: Professional Assessments for Beginning Teachers. These changes reflected standards for teachers written by subject matter associations.[5]

Although PRAXIS can be used to determine whether teachers have a firm grasp of their content area, some teachers may find themselves unable to plan and present an effective lesson—an untested area of preparation. Similarly, some teachers will be challenged by the administrative demands of the job beyond the classroom, such as recordkeeping, whereas others will encounter public relations problems within the context of their job descriptions. Even mature and accomplished teachers need some form of supervision, if only as a benchmark for further growth and achievement, but their accountability plans are not the plans of teachers with recognized problems. In short, professional accountability and supervision have as many faces as the teachers charged with their attainment.

Teachers are members of a diverse professional group. They come to the classroom with a wide range of professional preparation and an equally wide range of training and personal opinion on how best to execute the responsibilities of a public school teacher. Nevertheless, the systems now in place to ensure professional accountability assume that one instrument, one process, one definition of effectiveness will be equally applicable to every teacher.

Current methods for measuring professional effectiveness actually treat teachers as anything but true professionals. Their unique strengths, weaknesses, and needs are sacrificed to bureaucratic efficiency and collectively bargained equity. As a result, nine times out of ten, the accountability system misses the mark. Real needs go unaddressed, and the perception of all involved is that of only going through the motions of assessing accountability.

This text is premised on the idea that professional accountability and supervision plans, like professional growth plans, should be differentiated (i.e., that the focus, method and ultimate goal of any plan should be tailored to the job description and needs of the individual teacher). To illustrate this differentiated approach, the text presents different teacher and employee profiles and proposes different ways to supervise teacher and employee performances. Each model is introduced by a biographical scenario of a teacher likely to need and benefit from the particular model's approach. The problems that the models address cover the spectrum of issues that administrators and teachers encounter in getting the job done effectively, and the common thesis throughout is that no one plan for supervising and evaluating teachers fits all.

In addition, the text looks at methods for supervising administrative and specialized support staff, media specialists, guidance counselors, principals, assistant principals, school nurses, coaches, and the sundry other noncertified professionals who play a role in creating effective educational environments. Too often, the success or failure of schools is incorrectly presumed to rest solely with teachers. Schools, however, are really the sum of all of their parts. Every employee within a school plays a role in creating the learning environment that will determine ultimate success or failure of the school's mission. It should never be forgotten that schools are really publicly owned businesses, and, as such, no member of this public enterprise should be immune from supervision and accountability to the community served.

NOTES

1. G.W. Bracey, "Culture, Class, and Achievement," *Phi Delta Kappan 76*, no. 8 (1995): 647.
2. S. Black, "How Teachers Are Reshaping Evaluation Procedures," *Educational Leadership 50*, no. 6 (1993): 38–42.
3. J. Rooney, "Teacher Evaluation: No More 'Super'vision," *Educational Leadership 51*, no. 2 (1993): 43–44.
4. M.W. McLaughlin, "Embracing Contraries: Implementing and Sustaining Teacher Evaluation," in *The New Handbook of Teacher Evaluation: Assessing Elementary and Secondary School Teachers*, eds. J. Millman and L. Darling-Hammond (Newbury Park, CA: Sage Publications, 1990), 408.
5. A. Bradley, "Tests to Reflect New Teachers' Subject Savvy," *Education Week 19*, no. 9 (1999): 1.

Supervision: A Legal Perspective

1

Supervision:
A Legal Perspective

Employment accountability often comes down to a question of rights versus responsibilities—an employee's right to retain a position because a district has not fulfilled its responsibility to supervise and remediate performance as prescribed by law, contract, or board of education regulation. A significant trend has developed within the accountability movement, placing the onus for remediating teachers in trouble on school district administrators. A remediation requirement emerged with the interpretation of tenure statutes from the late 1970s, and, in the 1990s, interpretation of evaluation statutes appears to have intensified the trend to make remediation an issue in nonrenewal and dismissal proceedings.[1] Indeed, prescriptions for remediation can be found in state tenure statutes, in state evaluation statutes, in negotiated contracts, and in local board of education policies. Remediability is a jurisdictional question.[2] Thus, although not every state has a remediation requirement as a prerequisite for teacher nonrenewal or dismissal, there is a growing number of states and/or local boards of education, or negotiated teacher contracts that do.

Remediation makes both pedagogical and ethical sense. Faced with teacher shortages, it behooves school districts to rehabilitate employees with remediable problems and to give those who've taken the time and effort to train to be teachers a chance to attain their career goals and to succeed. Remediation is formal notice of recognized problems and targeted assistance in overcoming recognized short-comings in performance. Where there is a statute, contract clause, or board policy speaking to the issue of remediation, the courts will look for evidence that both the form and substance of the mandate to remediate have been addressed. The point of the requirements for remediation is positive—school boards and their administrators are forced to find out what is being taught in their classrooms and how it is being taught.[3] The purpose of evaluations is to assist teachers in improving.[3] The club that exists to force school districts to perform evaluations properly does not mean that evaluations exist only to initiate the removal of bad teachers.[3] Evaluations should be viewed as forms of summative commentary, giving teachers formal notice of areas needing attention—areas of concern that could give rise to discipline or dismissal. Formative supervision, on the other hand, is informal, actual remediation occurring over a period of time, and true remediation is the only way to avoid the costly litigation likely to accompany disputed dismissal or discipline proceedings.

NOTICE, ASSISTANCE, AND TIME TO IMPROVE

An essential part of any remediation requirement is *notice*. Federal due process (in education cases) requires that the teacher be given notice and an opportunity to be heard prior to termination.[4] Giving notice of remedial causes is, as noted earlier, jurisdictional, and the failure of a school board to give such a warning when called for prevents it from acquiring jurisdiction to discharge a teacher.[2] That is, employees must be told what they are doing wrong before districts can fire or discipline them. Notice is the first step in any remediation process. Common sense and fair play dictate that teachers must be told what they are doing wrong if they are to be able to improve. The failure to give proper notice of an unsatisfactory performance rating is grounds to nullify an unsatisfactory rating, even though the undisclosed rating, if properly announced, would have justified denial of tenure or dismissal from employment.[5] Knowing what needs correction is the first step in correcting unacceptable performance and is an integral part of according due process to any employee.

Once notice has been established, court scrutiny will turn to statutory requirements defining the course of remediation. In Missouri, for example, a three-step process is mandated:[6]

1. warning for behaviors that might result in charges;
2. a meeting and conference to remediate objectionable behaviors; and
3. formal charges.

Boards that fail to follow the procedures prescribed by law, contract, or their own policies risk having their efforts to discipline or dismiss reversed in court.[7] Many statutes and policies require that some form of actual assistance be given, ranging from an instructive postconference to an actual written plan of improvement. It is important that, when remediation is mandated by law, contract, or policy, school districts respond with the required degree of specificity. The Supreme Court has clearly stated that rules and regulations promulgated by an administrative agency (such as a school district) cannot be waived, suspended, or disregarded in a particular case, as long as such rules and regulations remain in force.[8] Thus, remediation procedures in state statutes and local policies must be followed closely.

Giving a teacher a one-page list of reference books to read came nowhere near the relief contemplated by a Louisiana remediation statute.[9] Also, an Ohio dismissal was overturned because the teacher had been observed only twice in the school year in question, with one observation lasting significantly less than 30 minutes,[7] despite the fact that Ohio law requires local boards to evaluate teachers (twice) after two 30-minute observations in each semester and to provide written recommendations for improvement within stated time lines.[10]

Remediation provisions, such as Ohio's, frequently provide time lines for improvement requirements for a specific number of observations and timely evaluations to monitor progress. Observations are the next step in the supervisory process. Time to improve also often becomes an issue in deciding whether a teacher with problems has been treated fairly. State statutes and court rulings underscore the need for both notice and time to respond. In *Board of Education v. State Board of Education*, the court found a warning followed by 15 days for remediation to be inadequate time to address a teaching deficiency.[11] However, in *Community Unit School District No. 60 v. Maclin*, another court found that 41 days is sufficient time for remediation.[12]

State statutes sometimes delineate the length of the remediation period following official notice of a problem. For example, Section 44938 of the *California Code* requires a remediation period of 45 calendar days for both suspensions and dismissals. Arizona[13] and New Jersey,[14] in contrast, require a 90-day opportunity to correct inadequacies. Some other state codes are more ambiguous regarding the length of the remediation period. Minnesota, for example, merely provides for discharge at the end of the school year after notice and remedial time,[15] and West Virginia requires simply an improvement period for behavior that is correctable.[16] Where statutes, regulations, or board policies do exist and provide specific direction, the courts will require district administrators to heed that direction or to lose dismissal and disciplinary actions where a teacher's behavior is deemed to be correctable.[17] Thus, it is important that supervisors become familiar with state statutes affecting teacher supervision, evaluation, discipline, and dismissal, and that they follow the mandated procedures to the letter. Supervisors must also heed any contract provisions addressing the course of notice and remediation. In some states, collectively bargained contracts will supersede state laws defining procedures for remediation.[18]

RANK AND RIGHTS

The employment rights of teachers depend in part on the terms of their initial appointment (probationary, temporary, or substitute teacher), in part on their subsequent work record and employment rank, and in part on individual and collectively negotiated contracts.[19] If a teacher is tenured, the teacher has a property right to retain a position unless dismissed for just cause, as defined by state law.[20] Tenured teachers have greater legal protections than do probationary, temporary, or substitute teachers. However, even nontenured, probationary, temporary, or substitute teachers may defend their right to employment by invoking claims of discrimination, unequal protection, or liberty abridgement. Both nontenured and tenured employees should be expected to take the position that the best defense is a good offense when faced with discipline or job loss. They will claim, rightly or wrongly, that they were disciplined, nonrenewed, or fired, not because of poor performance, but rather because of racial, religious, gender, age, or disability discrimination, or because they engaged in constitutionally protected activity found to be objectionable by the district. Threatened employees can be expected to claim that potential dismissal is actually employer retaliation for union activity or controversial expression on matters of public concern, constitutionally protected speech, and liberty interests. Such liberty and equal protection interests are created by federal—not state—laws, including the First and Fourteenth Amendments, as well as Title VII, Title IX, the Americans with Disabilities Act, and the Age Discrimination in Employment Act; these federal rights cannot be overruled by state law, contract, or district policy.

EFFECTIVE SUPERVISION: A RESPONSE TO LITIGATION

Informed supervisors need not fold in the face of a federal challenge. Effective supervision is its own defense to litigation based on claims of discrimination or retaliation for the exercise of constitutionally protected liberties. The courts have consistently supported documented district attempts to hold employees accountable for job performance. Case law protects the administrator who has supervised well. In such lawsuits, the burden of proof is always on the plaintiff employee, and a defending employer (i.e., supervisor) must be able to show merely that the driving force behind dismissal or discipline is documented proof of poor performance.

A defending school administrator is under no obligation to prove that the reason for the employment action given is legitimate and nondiscriminatory.[21] It is the complaining teacher who must prove that the reason (for discipline or dismissal) given is a lie and that the reason for the lie is intentional discrimination.[22] Essentially, to win a lawsuit charging discrimination, the teacher plaintiff must prove that the defending school board is lying about the teacher's performance and that the reason for the lie is discrimination. The burden of proof in cases alleging constitutional violations at all times remains with the plaintiff teacher/employee.

It should also be noted that, even if the plaintiff teacher were to succeed in proving that discrimination played a motivating part in the dismissal or disciplinary action taken, the school district can still avoid liability by proving that it would have made the same decision even if it had not allowed the discriminatory factor to play a role in the process.[23] Essentially, as long as district supervisors can show valid reasons for the dismissal/disciplinary action taken (i.e., as long as they've done their homework), not even a proven charge of discrimination can defeat their right as employers to control performance in the workplace. The Supreme Court has said that Title VII preserves an employer's freedom of choice; an employer shall not be liable if it can prove by a preponderance of evidence that, even if it had not taken the discriminatory factor into account, it would have acted in the same way.

For example, in *Mt. Healthy City School District v. Doyle*,[24] the Supreme Court instructed the lower court to determine whether the school board would have reached the same decision to fire plaintiff teacher Doyle in the absence of his exercise of protected provocative speech. Doyle, a teacher with a record of vulgar workplace outbursts and fighting, had telephoned a local radio station to voice his objections to a teacher grooming code. The Court reasoned that liberty interests such as protected speech should not place an employee such as Doyle in a better or worse position regarding continued employment. If, indeed, a school district can show a legitimate reason for disciplining or discharging a teacher, that legitimate reason should not be obscured by the teacher's unrelated liberty interests. In other words, a teacher with a record of poor performance should not be able to elude disciplinary action by merely evoking First Amendment or other liberty interests with provocative speech or behavior.

In essence, if school districts can show legitimate, documented reasons for the actions they take, the courts will support them, despite discrimination and liberty interest claims. With this in mind, the importance of documented supervision should be obvious. Documented supervision should include evidence of notice, assistance, and improvement monitoring over time. Evaluation alone is merely a single summative judgment call, easily challenged by charges of discrimination. Without supervisory documentation of problems cited, assistance offered, and time allotted for improvement, school districts risk falling prey to unfounded discrimination suits designed to weaken or defeat their attempts to call poor performance into question.

It should be noted that the case law cited does not apply only to teachers. The defense outlined above applies to any school employee who would claim discriminatory or liberty interest motives as the "real" reason for disciplinary response to poor performance. Few, if any, employees threatened by discipline or dismissal will go quietly into the night. Remember, they are not merely losing the job at hand. They are also acquiring a sullied work record that could keep them from getting the next job. Thus, they will, rightly or wrongly, use whatever means they can to shift the onus of failure from themselves to their employer. It therefore becomes increasingly important for supervisors to understand their own rights and responsibilities within the legal system governing employment practice and to act responsibly in asserting employer rights through clear, consistent, and continuous supervisory practices that comply with the letter of legislation, policy, or contract provisions defining their responsibilities in the employment accountability process.

The fact is that firing or disciplining any teacher, tenured or non-tenured, is not easy, nor should it be. The effect of such employment actions can destroy careers developed through years of study and personal sacrifice. Thus, boards of education and school administrators must be prepared for the time, effort, and legal costs that will be invested in defending decisions to nonrenew or dismiss. Even disciplinary action short of dismissal is likely to result in a grievance action that may, if contract states, require arbitration to reach resolution. This being said, it is, nevertheless, unconscionable to ignore poor performance that victimizes children simply because rooting it out is likely to be difficult. It is the job of ethical school districts and the administrators who represent them to bring poor performance to the fore and either to improve it or to root it out.

By the same token, it is important that teachers in every category believe that they are being treated fairly. Although due process is required before taking disciplinary action against tenured teachers, the elements of due process can go a long way in ensuring that the basic precepts of fairness are accorded every employee, regardless of rank, position, and job security interests. Specifically, if districts hope to avoid a day in court, every employee in trouble should be given notice of unsatisfactory performance and an opportunity to improve with assistance if, indeed, the area of concern is remediable. If the cause of concern is remediable, the dismissal action cannot continue until remediation has been addressed; if the cause is not remediable, the dismissal action may continue without a remediation period.[25] The question then becomes one of determining the difference between remediable and irremediable actions.

REMEDIABLE VERSUS IRREMEDIABLE BEHAVIOR

The test for determining remediable behavior asks three questions:

1. Were students, faculty, or schools damaged?
2. Could the conduct resulting in damage have been corrected, had the teacher been warned?[26]
3. Can the effects of the conduct in question be corrected?[27]

In separating remediable from irremediable causes, sexual impropriety, criminal activity, theft, and unethical conduct seem never to be remediable.[1] Incompetence, on the other hand, seems always to be remediable.[1] It should, however, be noted that, whereas conduct occurring once would usually be remediable, conduct occurring repeatedly over time can become irremediable.[1]

Courts will also look at how the behavior in question impairs a teacher's effectiveness. Eight factors are used to determine whether a teacher's effectiveness is impaired:

1. age/maturity of students;
2. likelihood that a teacher's conduct will adversely affect students or teachers;
3. degree of anticipated adversity;
4. proximity or remoteness in time of conduct;
5. extenuating or aggravating circumstances surrounding conduct;
6. likelihood that conduct may be repeated;
7. motives underlying conduct; and
8. whether conduct will have a chilling effect on rights of teachers.[28]

These parameters should be used by districts when determining whether supervision or dismissal is warranted by questionable teacher behavior.

The supervision models described in this text can be used to provide remediation, when called for, tailored to differentiated teacher/employee needs and circumstances. The models will also provide a paper trail of the due process requirements accorded a teacher in trouble, i.e., notice and remediation. The initial data collection identifies the problem and justifies the selection of one supervision model over another, whereas subsequent records note assistance provided and monitor progress made within a given period of time. Ideally, the model selected will help a teacher to correct cited concerns, but if it doesn't, the data gathered in implementing a given model can also serve as evidence of irremediable behavior justifying discipline or dismissal. The models serve both a practical and a philosophical purpose. They help supervisors to do the right thing for teachers and give them a written record of their efforts to do so.

SUPERVISION IN THE COURTS

Clarity, compliance, consistency, and continuity are key elements in winning disciplinary actions in arbitration or in court. *Clarity* simply means that notice and suggestions or plans for remediation should be straightforward, specific, and written. Any personnel evaluation system that does not clearly communicate to an employee those areas considered to be unsatisfactory performance does not afford an employee the due process required and is defective.[29]

Compliance refers to the need to know whatever statute, policy, or contract provision may govern supervision in a given instance and to follow the mandates of that provision to the letter. Failure to comply with the statutory requirements for remediation and evaluation constitutes a ground upon which a court can reverse a board's decision not to reemploy.[7]

Consistency refers to a district's efforts to treat all similarly situated employees in the same way. Discrimination and retaliation suits are often won on a finding of inconsistent policy application. That is, all employees with problems must be given notice and specific directions for addressing problems cited. Districts that single out one employee with problems while ignoring other employees with obvious problems are likely to lose if suit is brought. Once again, the best defense is a good offense, and employees threatened by discipline or dismissal can support claims of discrimination and retaliation by showing that they have been singled out for supervision when others equally merited closer monitoring and discipline but received neither.

Continuity is also an important part of effective supervision and a vital element of legal accountability. Courts will review what has gone before in determining the legitimacy of what is later claimed. Evaluations should connect to each other and to intervening supervision, and should reflect both present and prior concerns. That is, no supervisory visit should occur in a vacuum. Supervisors should review prior observations and evaluations to monitor progress in areas of concern. To comply with remediation statutes, evaluators should incorporate by reference earlier written reports that the teacher who is being supervised has seen.[30] Data gathered in observations and subsequent reports and evaluations should show a reasonable connection to each other and to final evaluations. Was there improvement in performance? Were concerns cited in earlier reports adequately addressed? If, indeed, progress has been made, that should be noted in subsequent observations and evaluations. If no progress was made, that, too, should be noted.

A teacher's evaluation must be based on observations of classroom performance and data gathered during those observations. It is difficult, if not impossible, to reconcile observations documenting problems with subsequent "glowing" evaluations that ignore prior concerns, and it is equally difficult to reconcile observations documenting "no problems" with subsequent poor evaluations implying continuous poor performance. Supervisors must analyze data gathered in each observation and read what they have written in earlier observations before they proceed with either the remediation or the evaluation process. This is more than a matter of form or expediency. It is simply a common-sense way to gauge progress in any remediation process and to ensure that teachers are treated fairly.

Lack of continuity can be another significant factor in defeating a district's case for discipline or dismissal. Plaintiff teachers, for example, can use observations and evaluations that do not relate to each other to show that the supervisor did not adequately supervise over time, and they can claim that the lack of continuity in the remediation process establishes a case for ambiguous, ineffective notice and ineffective remediation.

CASE STUDIES IN CLARITY, COMPLIANCE, CONSISTENCY, AND CONTINUITY

In this section, case fact patterns are presented, illustrating legal problems that districts have encountered in disciplining or dismissing teachers for poor performance. The subtitles indicate the particular problem addressed by the fact pattern that follows, and guidance is provided for avoiding future problems in dealing with this issue. The reader should try to recognize how the district got in trouble and to identify a prescriptive plan of action that might have avoided the day in court that resulted.

Clarity

Following a first observation, a teacher's supervisor noted that the teacher needed improvement in establishing and maintaining class control, but the supervisor stated that the teacher was improving in this area and gave the teacher an overall satisfactory rating. In a later observation, this same supervisor gave the teacher a rating of "needs improvement," specifically referring to lesson planning and using instructional methods and materials in conducting lessons. Despite this rating, the supervisor also noted that "improvement is noticeable."

In a third observation, the same supervisor again assigned the teacher an overall rating of "needs improvement," specifically citing the areas of class control, utilization of time, planning instruction, and use of a variety of teaching methods and techniques. Another supervisor observed the teacher on a fourth and fifth occasion and concluded that the teacher's work was "satisfactory" in every category. Despite these varying commentaries on the teacher's performance, the decision not to renew the teacher's contract was made, and that decision was subsequently contested.

Although the court in this case upheld the board's decision not to renew the teacher's contract, the dissent offers an opinion that should serve as a warning to supervisors regarding clarity.[29] The dissenting judge noted that the overall evaluation rating is ambiguous and that the evaluation document as a whole shows the overall evaluation to be satisfactory.[29] The dissent goes on to say that any ambiguity in employment actions must be construed against the school board.[29]

There is instructive wisdom in judicial dissents. Dissenting opinions often signal concerns that could ultimately defeat a winning position on appeal. Here, the concern is obvious ambiguity. One supervisor perceives the teacher's performance as needing improvement; the other perceives the same teacher's performance as satisfactory. The supervisor noting the need for improvement, however, cites decidedly different areas of concern each time the teacher is observed. At first, improvement was needed in establishing and maintaining class control. Next, improvement was needed in lesson planning and use of a variety of teaching methods and techniques. Then class control, utilization of time, planning instruction, and use of a variety of teaching methods and techniques became remediation issues. There was no clear statement of concern from the first supervisor, and the second supervisor gave the teacher satisfactory ratings in every category. The dissenting judge in this opinion went on to say that, although the majority interpreted "needs improvement" to mean that the employee's behavior is unsatisfactory, the dissent interpreted "needs improvement" to mean that the supervisor would like to see the employee improve a specific skill—a remediable issue.

Compliance

A state statute provided that a board of education must twice yearly evaluate teachers under limited contracts (nontenured teachers) before the board may determine whether to renew those teachers' contracts. One evaluation was to be completed by January 15 and the second by April 1. Each evaluation was to be based on two observations, with each observation lasting at least 30 minutes. The teacher disputing nonrenewal was observed only twice, and the observations were of less than 30 minutes.[3]

On appeal, the decision to nonrenew this teacher's contract and a lower court's finding that "the statutory requirements were substantially complied with" were overturned. The state Supreme Court in this case noted that the failure of the board to comply with the observation requirements of the law constituted a failure to comply with the evaluation requirements of the law[3] and that such a compliance failure constituted grounds for reversing the board's decision not to reemploy the teacher.

Never assume that "substantial" compliance with law, contract, or policy will be acceptable in court. Substantial compliance always raises the question of where the line between compliance and noncompliance should ultimately be drawn. When laws, contracts, and policies incorporate specific numbers into procedures, it is likely that adverse opinions will be appealed and that, in the final analysis, triers of fact will find that they cannot ignore legislated specificity.

Consistency

In an age-discrimination suit, the plaintiff teacher demonstrated that other, younger teachers with deficiencies similar to hers were retained by the district.[30] A 39-year-old female received eight "memos of concern" for such administrative infractions as forgetting to attend a meeting with the principal, incorrectly filling out an absence form, forgetting to sign the in/out log, permitting students to play cards during school, failing to provide the list of students outside of class when a fire alarm sounded, and arriving late for class. Another female aged 38 received seven "memos of concern" citing her failure to phone in her absence by a designated time, to submit an updated meeting agenda, to fill out absence forms correctly, and to provide comments for students receiving grades of D or F. These teachers, who were less than 45—the age of the plaintiff—were all rehired and received tenure, whereas the plaintiff was terminated.

On the other hand, a 52-year-old female teacher was the oldest of the teachers terminated and had fewer deficiencies than did any of the younger female teachers granted tenure. She had received only one memo of concern regarding student supervision but was, nevertheless, notified that her performance was such as to jeopardize her rehire and tenure.

This case illustrates administrative inconsistency in supervision practice. It should be noted that the court in this case found that, viewing the plaintiff teacher's evidence in its entirety and according her the benefit of favorable inferences, it could not say that a reasonable juror could not conclude that the defendant school district's proffered "legitimate, nondiscriminatory" reasons for not rehiring the plaintiff were pretextual. Thus, the lower court's decision favoring the school district was reversed and remanded for further proceedings consistent with the higher court's opinion.[30]

Teachers with similar deficiencies must receive similar supervision. In addition, subsequent evaluations and discipline based on documented performance must be equitable if districts are to avoid charges of discrimination or liberty abridgement. All employees with similar problems must be treated in the same way, especially when termination is at issue, if school districts are to avoid charges of discrimination. This case clearly illustrates the consequences of not doing so.

Continuity

In a first evaluation, a teacher was told to:

1. construct more detailed lesson plans, including topics to be taught, objectives for the day, and any homework assigned;
2. spend time each day teaching techniques of Mystery and College Writing; and
3. assign some of the work now being done in class as homework to have time to cover the topics during class.

This first evaluation also contained specific recommendations concerning where the teacher could obtain assistance:

1. review the Mystery and College Writing curriculum in the graded course of study;
2. review available course outlines; and
3. have a discussion with the department chair.

In the teacher's second evaluation, the teacher's supervisor said, "In the performance checklist that I gave you in December, I indicated several concerns. I also made several specific suggestions in the first evaluation. I do not feel that you have made enough improvement for me to recommend that your contract be renewed." The teacher contested the nonrenewal.[31]

In finding for the school board in this case, the court noted that this paragraph in the second evaluation expressly incorporated by reference the specific recommendations for needed improvements and the means by which the teacher could obtain assistance in making those improvements listed in the teacher's performance checklist and first evaluation. The court found that it was clear that the principal had complied with state law requiring notice, remediation, and assistance, and that the teacher's performance remained an issue warranting disciplinary action.[31]

This case is a good example of how continuity can expedite disciplinary action. The supervisor followed up on suggestions made in the first evaluation as part of a documented plan for expected improvement. Documented continuity overcomes the claim that supervision was more a matter of form than substance or that the problems cited were trivial. The court in this case recognized that the supervisor had real, recorded concerns that were not addressed by the teacher.

CONCLUSION

Supervision is not simply a pedagogical process. Supervision is the heart and soul of legally prescribed remediation. In the last 20 years, it has become increasingly clear that litigation will be a controlling factor in how schools function. With this in mind, public school administrators must get beyond seeing employee supervision as an empty chore with little but ritualistic value. The form and substance of supervision practice will ultimately determine every employee's rights to a given position, as well as administrative effectiveness. In a climate of accountability, supervision will play a formidable role in determining the employment viability of all school employees, including administrators. Poor performance cannot be tolerated indefinitely. Poor performance must be improved or eliminated, and supervision is the only legally acceptable avenue for evaluating both employee and administrator effectiveness.

THEORY INTO PRACTICE ACTIVITIES

1. What does your state law say a district must do before disciplining or dismissing a teacher?
2. Do your teachers collectively bargain?
3. If your teachers collectively bargain, what does the contract say must happen before a teacher is disciplined or terminated?
4. Have any teachers in your district been terminated? If so, describe the circumstances and any problems that may have occurred.
5. Give examples of irremediable teacher behavior that has been in the recent national, state, or local news.
6. Interview a union building representative in your district and discuss this chapter's definition of remediable and irremediable behavior. Ask the building representative to give you examples of remediable behavior the union has defended.
7. Using the test for determining remediable behavior from this chapter's section on "Remediable versus Irremediable Behavior," describe if the examples given in Activity 6 comply.

8. What does the law in your state and your own local contract say about *time to improve?*
9. Check your own observations and evaluation for the elements of *clarity, compliance, consistency,* and *continuity* discussed in this chapter.
10. Interview a building administrator concerning the way *supervision* and *evaluation,* as discussed in this chapter, are used to monitor teacher performance.

NOTES

1. D. Dagley, Remediation in Teacher Termination (Paper presented at the annual meeting of the Education Law Association, Chicago, IL, November 1999), 7.
2. Aulwurm v. Board of Education, 367 N.E.2d 1337 (Ill. 1977).
3. Snyder v. Mendon-Union Local School District Board of Education, 661 N.E.2d 717 (1996).
4. Franceski v. Plaquemines Parish School Board, 772 F.2d 197 (5th Cir. 1985).
5. Longarzo v. Anker, 578 F.2d 469 (2d Cir. 1978).
6. *Vernon's Annotated Missouri Statutes,* 168.116, Subd. 2.
7. *See, e.g.,* Farmer v. Kelleys Island Board of Education, 594 N.E.2d 204 (Ohio Com. Pl. 1992); Snyder v. Mendon-Union Local School Board of Education, 661 N.E.2d 717 (Ohio 1996); Naylor v. Cardinal Local School District Board of Education, 630 N.E. 2d 725 (Ohio 1994).
8. United States ex rel Accardi v. Shaughnessy, 347 U.S. 260 (1954).
9. Gaulden v. Lincoln Parish School Board, 54 So.2d 152 (2d Cir. 1989).
10. *Ohio Revised Code,* § 3319.111.
11. 403 N.E.2d 27 (Ill. App. 1980).
12. 435 N.E.2d 845, (1982).
13. *Arizona Revised Statutes,* 15–538.
14. *New Jersey Statutes Annotated,* 18A: 6–11.
15. *Minnesota Statutes,* 125.12 Subd. 6.
16. *West Virginia Code,* 18A-2-8.
17. *See, e.g.,* Cox v. York County School District No. 083, 560 N.W.2d 138 (Neb., 1997); Board of Education Baltimore County v. Ballard, 507 A.2d 192 (Md. App. 1986); Childs v. Roane County Board of Education, 929 S.W.2d 364 (Tenn. App. 1996).
18. *See, e.g., Ohio Revised Code,* § 4117.10(A).
19. W.D. Valente, *Law in the Schools* (Upper Saddle River, NJ: Prentice-Hall, 1998), 86.
20. Bishop v. Wood, 416 U.S. 341 (1976).
21. Texas Department of Community Affairs v. Burdine, 450 U.S. 248 (1981).

22. St. Mary's Honor Center v. Hicks, 509 U.S. 502 (1993).

23. Price Waterhouse v. Hopkins, 490 U.S. 228 (1989).

24. 429 U.S. 282 (1977).

25. Ganyo v. Independent School District No. 832, 311 N.W.2d 497 (Minn. 1981).

26. Gilliland v. Board of Education, 365 N.E.2d 322 (1977).

27. Board of Education of Argo-Summit School District No. 104 Cook County v. Hunt, 487 N.E.2d 24 (Ill. App. 1 Dist. 1985).

28. Hoagland v. Mount Vernon School District 320, 623 P.2d 1156 (Wash. 1981).

29. McKenzie v. Webster Parish School Board, 653 So.2d 215 (La. App. 2 Cir. 1995).

30. Greenburg v. Camden County Vocational and Technical Schools, 708 A.2d 460 (1998).

31. Thomas v. Board of Education of Newark City School District, 643 N.E.2d 131 (1994).

2

An Overview of the Differentiated Supervision Process

An Overview of the Differentiated Supervision Process

DIFFERENTIATED SUPERVISION

T his approach to supervision emphasizes the "direct" and "differentiated" aspects of supervision. Classrooms and schools all differ in their focus and their demands, and teachers and other school employees all differ in their skills and their needs. Traditional evaluation plans can be legally and contractually limiting and structured, prescribing the conditions for evaluation, the length and number of observations, as well as the form and substance of conferences held. In contrast, differentiated supervision plans stress assistance to improve performance—not evaluation—and are individualized, tailored to the identified needs of specific teachers, staff, and situations. The number and length of observations, the way data are collected, and the frequency of conferencing will all vary with the individual employee's needs, the specific situation being monitored, and the model chosen for supervision.

Just as an Individual Education Plan is designed to address the performance needs of the individual student, so a Differentiated Supervision Plan should be developed to address an individual teacher or employee's professional performance needs. Supervisors will choose from the models presented on a case-by-case basis, relying on their own knowledge base, teacher or employee characteristics, recent observations, personal interactions with the teacher or employee, and their analysis of the current situation.[1] It is also vital that, in each instance, impressions noted and supervision choices made by the supervisor be supported by hard data collected in the course of working with the teacher in and out of the classroom. That is, there must be a documented reason supporting the choice of one supervision model over others. Differentiated Supervision Plans should never be a matter of "gut feelings" or assumptions, but rather the product of real facts and numbers—data observed and gathered—and should be shared with the teacher or employee at a given point. The goal is to provide reasoned and meaningful supervision for every adult employed in the school community.

Once such data have been collected, the next step in a Differentiated Supervision Plan is the careful analysis of the data and their impact on professional effectiveness. Which observed behaviors and consequences can be directly linked to the data collected, and what do these observed behaviors and consequences say about teacher and employee performance? This analysis will become the focal point for the mentoring and supervising conferences held following observations. Ideally, those supervised should receive copies of the data collected in advance of supervising conferences so that they can independently do a cause-and-effect analysis of their own professional performances before conferencing with supervisors. Just as good teachers strive to have students develop the ability to learn independently by analyzing the consequences of their own performances, so must good supervisors strive to have all school employees develop the ability to analyze their own performances and to plan for improvement and growth where needed.

The classroom is always the first focal point of school supervision because what happens in the classroom is the central focus of education. If there are areas of concern centering on classroom performance, these areas must be the first focus of supervision. If classroom performance is exemplary, the stage is set to expand the range of observation, opportunity, and professional accountability beyond classroom concerns.

Development of a plan for growth and improvement addressing specific areas of concern or interest is the next step integral to differentiated supervision in public schools. This improvement plan should evolve from the data collected and the analysis of that data discussed in the mentoring conference, and should offer specific suggestions for improving or expanding on existing performance outcomes. The improvement plan should also describe the specific ways in which improvement will be measured, i.e., how accountability for growth and improvement will be determined.

Finally, there should be additional observations to collect and analyze data after the improvement plan has been implemented in order to monitor the plan's ongoing effectiveness in addressing identified needs. Additional mentoring conferences should be held to discuss these observations and any need for an adjustment in the improvement plan. All steps in this supervisory process are designed to assist, but not yet formally assess, the school employee. Thus, improvement plans ideally are cooperatively created, rather than administratively mandated, whenever possible.

As educators well know, "telling" someone what to do is the least effective approach to learning. This is particularly true for adults. Adult learners have a great degree of self-directedness, have experiences that form a knowledge base, and learn by solving problems.[2] This plan for differentiated supervision builds on that self-directedness, past experience, and need to solve problems encountered in the course of professional performance.

Exhibit 2-1 summarizes the steps in the general process of differentiated supervision, but it must again be emphasized that what happens at each step of the process will be uniquely tailored to the identified needs of the individual school employee gathered through specific data collection and analysis. No two plans need be alike. Rather, each plan will evolve from the singular situation in which the employee and supervisor find themselves. Each such situation will have a different focus, forum, purpose, and panoply of options for addressing perceived needs and concerns. Supervisors and employees will work cooperatively to develop these individualized accountability plans.

Supervision of any kind has always been an unsettling concept for teachers and for all school employees. Teachers do not know whether to rely on the supervisor for support or to avoid the supervisor for fear of being criticized.[3] Some view supervision as a threat to professional autonomy; others see the process as empty ritual with little real effect on what they do. However, teachers who are not supervised feel isolated and undervalued.[4] All true professionals, however skilled, have the need to discuss what they do and to have ob-

Exhibit 2–1 The Process

Step	Action	Purpose
Step 1	Observe	To Assist
Step 2	Collect Data	To Identify Need(s)
Step 3	Analyze Data	To Verify Need(s)
Step 4	Create Supervision Plan	To Address Need(s)
Step 5	Collect Data Again	To Measure Effect of Plan
Step 6	Conference Again	To Adjust Plan
Step 7	Plan Maintenance	To Ensure Growth

jective commentary and assistance from time to time in validating the success of their efforts. Even those with no visible problems or concerns need outside confirmation of their perceived success and need help in discovering new ways to grow professionally. Supervision is not just for teachers in trouble. Supervision is benchmarking for professional growth, and all school employees, at all stages of their careers, need to assess regularly where they are in order to plan for where they want to be. Fullan said that educational change is a learning experience for the adults involved.[5] Supervision is the lesson plan for that learning experience—the path to professional growth, as well as to professional accountability. Without a plan, professional growth becomes a possibility, not a probability, and accountability becomes an empty promise.

TAKING SUPERVISION SERIOUSLY

Having distinguished supervision from evaluation, it becomes necessary to stress again the importance of *both* supervision and evaluation to successful school administration. School administrators have always perceived *evaluation* as important because it has always had legal implications, i.e., in most states, evaluation is legislatively required before awarding tenure and is used to justify termination of tenured teachers and employees who do not continue to perform as expected. Most states have laws, regulations, or guidelines regarding how teachers are to be evaluated[6] and have negotiated contracts to determine how other employees are to be evaluated. Only after a trial period in which teachers are observed and evaluated first-hand and found competent in their craft do they receive tenure status, i.e., a continuing contract, assuring them that they cannot be removed from their positions without demonstrated just cause. After receiving tenure, specific statutory grounds must be proven by a board of education before it can remove a teacher with a continuing contract. Thus, tenure equates with job security for teachers, and this job security emphasizes the importance of administrative evaluation, both before tenure and after tenure is awarded. In a similar way, most classified employee-negotiated contracts protect support staff from discipline or dismissal without just cause.

Procedures for evaluating nontenured and tenured teachers are in the foreground for administrators because they, too, are often part of the negotiated contract and are monitored by the teachers' unions. Although evaluation in many districts may amount to nothing more than going through the motions and paperwork as prescribed by contract, it is a task that administrators cannot legally or contractually ignore.

As noted, *supervision*, i.e., assistance in becoming a better teacher or nonteaching employee, on the other hand, has been only incidentally legislated, and that has happened primarily in the last 10 years. Many, but not all, states now require specific suggestions and, to a less frequent extent, a substantial period for remediation of teachers with problems.[7] Supervision and mentoring are the essence of remediation, but not until recently were they prescribed in any detail in either law or contract. Thus, supervision, a far more intensive and time-consuming task than evaluation, has been given short shrift by busy administrators preoccupied with the legislated and contractual deadlines for evaluation that *are* spelled out for them.

Lack of time is the red herring often proffered by administrators as a reason for sacrificing supervision to evaluation. Discipline, staffing, scheduling, budgeting, public relations, and evaluation all take precedence over supervision in the daily scheme of things, and many administrators believe that teachers who succeed in getting hired should not need help in doing what they've been hired to do.

It should be noted, however, that supervision has an undeniable impact on all other administrative tasks. Supervision, done well, will eliminate the discipline and academic problems that give rise to public relations problems. Teachers who teach well and also understand how to solve their own problems free an administrator to deal with more pressing issues of instructional leadership. Also, as intimidating a task as classroom supervision may seem at first sight, it, too, is manageable for the administrator who values it and builds it into the daily schedule. If each administrator were to supervise just one teacher each day, 180 opportunities would be available to help teachers become self-sustaining professionals. Surely, in a seven-period school day, the dedication of one period to the cause of supervision is not too much to ask.

WHO SHOULD SUPERVISE TEACHERS

Those 180 opportunities can be further increased if the range of persons eligible to supervise goes beyond the limited pool of building administrators. Supervision need not be the province of only the school administrator. Although traditionally and contractually, the authority to evaluate teachers has rested with the building principals, in recent years, others have come to play a significant role in the actual work of supervising teachers. That is, others have been recognized as valuable in supplying teachers with the data they need for feedback concerning their performances. Peer coaching, student proficiency testing, and parent surveying have all been used by districts and teachers to help supervise performance. In addition, in an age of technologic growth, teachers have had the opportunity to avail themselves of technical self-supervision using video- and audiotaping. In short, supervision need not be the province of any one person or group. In fact, the best supervision should really entail a variety of feedback sources. What better way to validate the concerns of an administrator or teacher than by showing that they are also the concerns raised by peer, parent, and student assessment of performance? The tendency to compartmentalize and limit supervisory feedback sources can actually sabotage opportunities to recognize needs and deal with concerns effectively. A single source of concern is seldom given the same attention as are multiple sources that repeatedly cite the same concern.

This is yet another way in which supervision must be differentiated from evaluation. The decision as to who may evaluate teachers and other school employees may, indeed, be limited by either law or contract. For example, in Ohio, only certified administrators may evaluate teachers unless the individual contract makes an exception.[8] Those who evaluate teachers will ultimately control the question of their continued employment, and the concern that evaluators be trained and certified is legitimate. Those who supervise teachers, however, are there to assist teachers, rather than to assess teachers for employment purposes. Supervisors provide feedback to teachers themselves and assist them in using this feedback to improve their performance before evaluation takes place. Evaluator feedback becomes part of a public record to be used to support employment decisions made on behalf of a school district.

Often, the most effective supervision is not administratively implemented. With training, each model presented in this text can be effectively used by administrators, peers, or teachers themselves to assist in the personal quest for differentiated supervision or reinforcement of successful practice. At present, too many administrators see themselves cast only in the role of evaluator, rather than evaluator and supervisor. To do so is to forego an opportunity to help teachers and administrators themselves attain a new level of professionalism.

WHAT SHOULD BE SUPERVISED

Evaluation will guide and inform supervision. Just as final exams should reflect the material that has been taught, so should every employee's evaluation throw a light on those aspects of job performance for which the employee will be accountable. Supervision does not occur in a vacuum. Evaluation instruments will illuminate the variety of factors that can become the subject of supervision, and the models presented in this text are each developed around a different focus for the supervision process. No one model suffices in all situations. Instead, each addresses a different situation in which teachers, employees, and supervisors may find themselves. The scenarios introducing each chapter serve to illustrate an example of the issue(s) addressed by each model. Focus and instructive data collection determine which model is selected to supervise in a given situation.

Exhibit 2-2 lists each model and briefly describes the focus for supervision and the type of problem that might be addressed by using the model. The examples given are but a sampling of the kinds of situations that give rise to the need for supervision and should not be viewed as definitive.

Exhibit 2–2 Supervision Models

Model	Focus	Example
Trait	Teacher Traits	Teacher Dress Issue
Process	Structure of Lesson	Poor Lesson Plan
Instructional Objectives	Student Learning	Poor Student Work
Teacher Performance Objectives	Teacher Performance out of Classroom	Teacher Tardiness
Peer Supervision	Professional Skills and Collegiality	Classroom Control
Self-Supervision	Teacher Concerns	Student Participants
Parent Supervision	Parent Perceptions	Parent Complaints
Student Supervision	Student Perceptions	Student Complaints
Certified Nonteaching Staff	Guidance, Nurse	Poor Record Keeping
Extracurricular Program Supervision	Advisors and Coaches	Problems and Controversies
Administrator Supervision	Principals and Other Administrators	Program Accountability
Support Staff Supervision	Secretaries, Custodians, etc.	Courtesy and Confidentiality
Student Teachers and Substitutes	Teaching Performance	Failure to Teach Effectively

As mentioned earlier, each chapter will begin with a scenario best addressed by the model to be discussed. Next, the theory, supervision method, means of data collection, data analysis, and conferencing unique to each model will be presented. In the "Theory into Practice" section of each chapter, students will have the opportunity to use each model's forms and procedures in either hypothetical or actual situations. They will also have the opportunity to react to each model's perceived effectiveness.

The goal of the text is to provide a repertoire of methods for supervising teachers and all school support personnel, both in and out of the classroom, as well as the training and insight to choose the method most likely to provide actual assistance in a given situation. The text will also discuss the administrative, contractual, and legal implications of using each model. Supervision, like evaluation, does not take place in a vacuum. Legislation, case law, and contract will all have an impact on the models and procedures adopted. Legislation, although purposefully passed, is never static. It is interpreted and clarified by the courts through case law and adapted to local needs and norms by board policy and the negotiated contract.

JOB DESCRIPTIONS AND ORIENTATION

Job descriptions are the starting points for any professional supervision or accountability program. For supervision or evaluation to be effective, each party engaged in either process must understand what a given position in the district entails. The job description becomes the basis for performance expectations and a template for accountability. The development of job descriptions is a vital first step in clearing away any ambiguities that might exist. Contracts further help to clarify what's expected—what an employee's working day will look like and what obligations for teachers beyond classroom teaching may exist. The clear delineation of rights, responsibilities, and lines of authority found in job descriptions serve both a practical and a legal purpose.

Practically speaking, no employer can expect an employee to anticipate what a job entails. There must be a clear statement of duties and responsibilities if the job is to be done as the employer wishes. Teachers cannot be expected to remain after school for extra help sessions if they've never been told that this is part of their contractual duties. Nor can they be expected to follow a curriculum that they've never been given or trained to implement. Common sense and fair play require that teachers and all employees, upon hiring, receive adequate notice of what they will be expected to do and how they will be expected to perform.

Job descriptions, contracts, teachers' handbooks, student handbooks, and curriculum guides are not optional equipment. They are legal necessities. Legally speaking, job descriptions, contracts, teachers' handbooks, student handbooks, and curriculum guides give employees *official notice* concerning what will be expected of them as they begin their work in a district. Districts that fail to provide such vital information not only sabotage their own efforts to run an orderly system, they also make it impossible to hold employees legally responsible for the job they've been hired to do. Courts have repeatedly shielded teachers from disciplinary action taken by districts that have failed in their own efforts to clarify their expectations for job performance.[9]

Orientation programs that provide both materials and training for newly assigned teachers and school employees take on great importance. The use of mentors as well as supervisors to clarify and reinforce job expectations will ensure that all employees are given the opportunity to succeed. Orientation programs should discuss the ways in which employees will ultimately be evaluated, emphasizing areas deemed particularly important by the district and building administrator. Forms and procedures for collecting and reporting data, and conferencing and providing assistance should be explained and shared in an effort to make teachers aware of the paper trail that will be used to monitor these job performance expectations.

CONCLUSION

Effective performance for every school employee is the product of both supervision and evaluation. Evaluation alone is an intimidating judgment call on performance and likely to be the focus of grievances and legal challenge. Utilizing evaluation together with supervision removes the sting and threat in such judgment calls by making advance guidance and assistance a part of the process.

THEORY INTO PRACTICE ACTIVITIES

1. Describe the procedures your district uses to evaluate teachers. Does it always follow these procedures? Explain.
2. Does your district or contract also prescribe procedures for supervising teachers?
3. Describe an occasion when you or a fellow teacher received supervision, as described in this chapter (i.e., *assistance* in improving performance).

4. Briefly describe your own reaction to your district's evaluation process. Do you fear, welcome, or ignore your principal's visit?
5. What would your response be to a bad evaluation? Why?
6. Find out how other teachers in your school react to evaluation. How would they react to supervision as described in this chapter?
7. What could your principal do to help you personally become a better teacher?
8. How often are you observed by others?
9. Have you ever been observed by another teacher?
10. Did you receive a job description and orientation when first hired? If not, develop a job description for your position.
11. How is the nonteaching staff in your building evaluated?
12. How are administrators in your building evaluated?
13. Review contract provisions dealing with evaluation for each of the employee groups appearing in Exhibit 2–2.
14. Review the job descriptions for each of the employees mentioned in Exhibit 2–2.
15. How often are these nonteaching employees evaluated?

NOTES

1. C.D. Glickman et al., *Supervision of Instruction: A Developmental Approach*. 4th ed. (Needham Heights, MA: Allyn & Bacon, 1998), 195.
2. M. Knowles, *Andragogy in Action: Applying Modern Principles of Adult Learning* (San Francisco, CA: Jossey-Bass, Publishers, 1984).
3. K.A. Acheson and M.D. Gall, *Techniques in the Clinical Supervision of Teachers*, 4th ed. (Reading, MA: Longman, 1997), 15.
4. G. Natriello and S.M. Dornbusch, "Pitfalls in the Evaluation of Teachers by Principals," *Administrator's Notebook 29* (1981): 1–4.
5. M.G. Fullan, *The New Meaning of Educational Change* (New York: Teachers College Press, 1991).
6. P.A. Zirkel, *The Law of Teacher Evaluation* (Bloomington, IN: Phi Delta Kappa Educational Foundation, 1996), 32–33.
7. Zirkel, *The Law of Teacher Evaluation*, 9.
8. *Ohio Revised Code*, § 3319.111(A).
9. *See, e.g.*, Mailloux v. Kiley, 323 F.Supp. 1387 (D. Mass. 1971), *affirmed*, 448 F.2d 1243 (1st Cir. 1971).

The Trait Model: Describing the Exemplary Teacher

- Model Traits of the Exemplary Teacher

- The Method
  - I. Define Desired Characteristics
  - II. Provide Forms and Procedures That Require Explanations and Recommendations
  - III. Train Teachers and Supervisors To Collect Data
  - IV. Conferencing

- Pros and Cons of the Trait Model

- Evaluating with the Trait Model: A Legal Perspective

- Theory into Practice Activities

The Trait Model: Describing the Exemplary Teacher

Pat is new to both teaching and Beacon Middle School. When interviewed, Pat appeared to be a very capable young math teacher, but Pat's principal has noticed that Pat has several disturbing habits. Pat ignores the faculty dress code outlined in the Teacher Handbook, arriving for work in jeans and sweat shirts, and Pat has been late for first period class several times.

MODEL TRAITS OF THE EXEMPLARY TEACHER

Many traits define the exemplary teacher. It goes without saying that knowledge of subject matter is an essential trait of an effective teacher.[1] However, simply knowing what to teach is not the same as knowing how to teach or projecting the confidence and concern that make learning possible. One need only think of the best teacher they've ever had to realize that many other personal and professional attributes define the effective teacher. The Trait Model assumes that good teachers and good teaching can be described in words or phrases that capture these special qualities, the characteristics of the successful educator. This approach to supervision grew out of the effective schools movement and is based on the assumption that most teachers and supervisors can develop serviceable definitions of effective teaching to guide the supervision process,[2] and, needless to say, many and varied serviceable definitions have evolved.

Two commercially marketed examples are *The Teacher Perceiver*[3] and *Praxis III.*[4] The Gallup Organization developed *The Teacher Perceiver,* an interview rubric identifying *themes,* recurring patterns of thought, feeling, and behavior believed to identify potentially successful teachers.[5] Trained interviewers look for evidence of these themes in applicant answers to questions about situations that they are likely to encounter as teachers. The Educational Testing Service's *Praxis III* is a supervision rubric for entry-year teachers identifying 19 essential criteria for effective teaching. *Praxis III*-trained supervisors observe entry-year teachers, collect data, and review and analyze the data, documenting the presence or absence of these criteria. These commercial examples of Trait Model supervision are tested and marketed examples of instruments that have been used in many school districts for a very long time.

Traits, no matter what they are called, are brief statements describing various aspects of teacher behavior in and out of the classroom. These traits become a template for assessing teacher performance and offering guidance where improvement is needed. A study of 272 randomly selected school districts indicated that 84 percent of the districts in this sample used some version of the Trait Model to supervise teachers.[6] The popularity of this supervision method appears to stem from the fact that required observer skills in most, but not all, models are limited, and the relatively simple nature of the instrument minimizes the need for close or frequent professional contact.[7] Most supervisors using this model assume that the traits listed on the instruments they use are self-explanatory. Unfortunately, this may be an unwarranted assumption in today's defensive and litigious educational climate.

THE METHOD

The trait supervision instrument can either merely indicate the presence or absence of a given trait or attempt to measure the extent to which a given trait has been observed. Exhibit 3–1 is a segment of

Exhibit 3–1 Presence or Absence of Traits

Characteristic	Yes	No
Knowledge of Subject		
Questioning Skill		
Rapport with Students		
Good Grooming		
Enthusiasm		

a typical Trait Model instrument in which the mere presence or absence of the trait is noted.

This segment of a Trait Model instrument exemplifies the simplest version of this approach, requiring the supervisor to note only whether there was or was not evidence of a given trait observed. The basis for the opinion registered need not be confined to the classroom setting, and, in this simplest of versions, there is no requirement to cite evidence supporting the judgment of the observer.

Exhibits 3–2 and 3–3 expand on this basic Trait Model instrument. Exhibit 3–2 provides a scale for indicating the degree to which a particular quality has been noted, and Exhibit 3–3 adds a column for briefly describing the basis on which judgment has been rendered regarding each characteristic.

Ideally, specific data should be collected and cited to support the observer's assessment. For example, in supervising Pat, the teacher in the opening scenario, the principal might support a marginal rating

Exhibit 3–2 Measuring Trait Presence

Characteristic	Strong	Satisfactory	Marginal
Planning Skill			
Voice Quality			
Classroom Control			
Professionalism			
Dependability			

Exhibit 3–3 Degree to Which Traits Are Observed and Justification

Characteristic	Strong	Satisfactory	Marginal	Evidence
Creativity				
Scholarship				
Patience				
Appearance				
Punctuality				

in the categories of appearance and punctuality with specific dates on which Pat came to work in jeans and sweat shirts and the dates on which Pat was late for the first class. These dates would provide the data supporting use of this model to supervise Pat's behavior and could also include written remarks or reprimands to Pat regarding dress and lateness. The model would be used similarly by supervisors who have collected data focusing on other listed teacher traits.

As Figure 3–1 shows, numerical gradients can also be used to indicate the degree to which a particular characteristic has been observed; again, instruments may require separate explanations and specific data supporting a poor or marginal rating on the instrument.

In its simplest forms, the Trait Model is basically an *assessment* instrument, in that it provides no data supporting the judgments made, nor any place for suggestions on ways to improve or enhance performance. There are, however, ways in which even the basic Trait Model can become a *supervision* tool, providing guidance and data-supported feedback and assistance.

I. Define Desired Characteristics

Researchers who have compared the content of Trait Model Instruments have found that there is no general agreement as to what constitutes the essential characteristics of a competent teacher and that the items on rating scales tend to be subjective, undefined, and varied.[8] Preobservation guidance defining the traits of an effective teacher is the first step in making this model supervisory, evaluative, and assistive, as well as assessive. To ensure this, teachers are given written definitions of traits with relevant examples of satisfactory and unsatisfactory performance. Videotapes graphically illustrating superior, acceptable, and unacceptable behavior can also be helpful. Essentially, the supervisor becomes a "teacher of teachers" by provid-

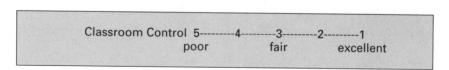

Figure 3–1 Trait Model with Numerical Gradient

ing teachers with a literal and visual definition of performance expectations.

One recognized drawback of the Trait Model in its simpler forms is its subjectivity. Even with rating scales, the Trait Model remains highly subjective. Ratings depend on:

1. what each rater thinks the teacher ought to be doing;
2. what behaviors were taken into account;
3. the weight attached to each behavior observed; and
4. the reference standard used to arrive at the rating.[9]

Thus, without some effort at standardization and data gathering, ratings will vary from observer to observer, and the teacher's own perception of what each characteristic entails will add to the confusion. A virtual Tower of Babel can be created if terms and conditions are not adequately defined and illustrated before the fact so that all can understand what's expected and how ratings will be determined. Therefore, the first step in making the Trait Model a useful supervisory instrument is to define its terms as clearly and objectively as possible. What does it mean to have *knowledge of subject matter, rapport with students, enthusiasm,* or any other of the qualities that routinely appear on the Trait Model forms? What specific examples can be given of observable, measurable behavior documenting success or reason for concern in one of these areas? How will the supervisor distinguish serious from trivial problems? How will the observer distinguish satisfactory from superior performance?

To illustrate this point, let us consider the trait *knowledge of subject matter.* In one instance, the supervisor observes a mathematics class in which a teacher is modeling the solution of a word problem and makes a simple computational error in the course of the solution that results in an incorrect answer. An observant student catches the error and brings it to the teacher's attention, but only after five minutes have elapsed with the teacher wondering aloud why the solution didn't work. In another instance, a teacher conducting a spelling lesson repeatedly misspells one of the words being taught in the lesson. Obviously, the second example is more indicative of a teacher with knowledge of subject matter problems. The math teacher's shortcomings are more a matter of attention to detail, rather than actual failure to know the subject. The fact that a student was able to recognize the computational error could, with teacher *experience* and *creativity*, be used by the teacher to build student initiative and encourage attentiveness. On the other hand, the spelling teacher's repeated failure to recognize self-made spelling errors presents a far more serious concern. The spelling teacher is disseminating incorrect information, and, by virtue of the teacher's role authority and the students' intellectual immaturity, students are not likely to question the teacher's incorrect presentation. Repeated error indicates that the spelling teacher does not know the subject matter being taught. In defining the characteristics used in the Trait Model, such examples can be very helpful ways of illustrating the difference between unsatisfactory and acceptable performance in a given subject area.

Examples should also be given to illustrate the difference between satisfactory and superior teaching. Satisfactory performance might be illustrated by a teacher who presents only a one-dimensional lesson, i.e., a lesson in which material is presented through lecture alone. In contrast, superior teachers would be expected to use a variety of learning modalities in developing a topic because superior teachers realize that students have different learning styles. Superior teachers also have the deep understanding of their subject that allows them to present it through a variety of stimulating activities. The satisfactory teacher uses a simple, direct, and, therefore, "satisfactory" format in developing a lesson. A superior teacher develops techniques and activities that challenge as well as present and reinforce. The superior teacher makes certain that critical thinking skills are developed in every lesson. Today's educators are far too willing to accept mediocrity masquerading in the guise of excellence. The system has grown accustomed to being satisfied with adequate but uninspired teaching. Proponents of the Trait Model have an excellent opportunity to distinguish mediocrity from excellence and to identify each officially as it appears in the classroom experience.

Once again, specific examples should be given to illustrate the difference between satisfactory and superior performance. A satisfactory spelling lesson, for example, is one in which the teacher correctly places all new spelling words on the board, defines them, and uses them correctly in a sentence. A superior spelling lesson is one in which the teacher has the students first read a story in which all the new words appear, then places the new words on the board and asks students to write sentences defining the new words from the context of the story and to draw pictures illustrating their meaning to be used in a contest in which fellow students will label each drawing with the spelling word that the picture illustrates.

Defining characteristics to be used in supervising teachers through example has a twofold benefit. Not only do teachers better understand the basis for judgments that will be made, but they also receive indirect instruction on how to structure and improve their performance. This preliminary and indirect instruction converts the Trait Model from an *assessment instrument* to an *assisting tool*. Teachers are not stupid. When they realize what it will take to rise above mediocre performance, they are more likely to strive to do just that. Part and parcel of what a successful supervisor does is to help teachers discern the superior from the mediocre approach to teaching. Schools have an obligation to become more like teaching hospitals, structuring experiential teaching and learning opportunities for neophytes and veterans in the profession.

Creation of a videotape to model performance that is marginal, satisfactory, and excellent is yet another way to learn and teach through the supervisory process itself. Supervisors charged with depicting the types of visible measurable data that would justify each rating that they give will have a better idea of what they themselves are looking for during an observation and how the degree to which a particular trait appears will be determined. The process of preparing such orientation materials serves the purpose of forcing supervisors to clarify in their own minds how they will gather data to substantiate the opinions that they will render in mentoring conferences and on the Trait Model forms used to supervise. Such orientation to a trait system of supervision becomes an assisting tool for both supervisors and teachers that will, in the long term, save time and energy arguing with a teacher about an observer's subjective concerns and ratings.

II. Provide Forms and Procedures That Require Explanations and Recommendations

Forms and written procedures can be developed to ensure that the Trait Model is used as an effective supervisory tool. If supervisors are required to collect and report data to support their recorded perceptions, they will, in the course of collecting the data, bring real problems to the teacher's attention. Exhibits 3–4 and 3–5 illustrate how such a Trait Model Instrument can be used successfully to require administrators to inform and assist before problems become a focus for evaluation.

To give the teacher a marginal rating in the area of punctuality, the supervisor would have to provide data and notice documenting lateness. Formal documentation requires the supervisor to speak with the teacher or write the teacher a memo, formally recognizing instances of lateness. In this case, the supervisor has referred to an attached memo to the teacher (Exhibit 3–5). The memo was sent to

---

Exhibit 3–4 Trait Model Form for Supervision

Indicate the degree to which you have observed a given trait in or out of the classroom. Whenever a rating of less than satisfactory is assigned, justify the rating by attaching supportive data from your observation and provide written guidance for improvement.				
Trait	*Marginal*	*Satisfactory*	*Excellent*	*Data*
Punctuality	X			See Memo

Exhibit 3–5 Data Supportive to Trait Model Form for Supervision

MEMO

October 19, 1998

TO: Pat Smith

FROM: Chris Shore

RE: Lateness to Work

Dear Pat,

It has come to my attention that you were late to your class three times this week. Specifically, your class was left unattended on October 16, 17, and 18 for five minutes at the start of first period. Please do not let this happen again. Your lateness poses a concern for student safety as well as learning. If there is a problem and I can in any way assist you, please see me as soon as possible. If there is no problem, I will assume that you will take care that your class not be left unattended again.

the teacher before the Trait Model form was completed but serves as documentation of an observed problem with punctuality, a trait that appears on the supervisory form.

Knowing that documentation will be required for marginal ratings, supervisors are more likely to bring concerns to a teacher's attention when they occur, thus assuring objectivity and ample time to correct marginal behavior, as well as a documented record of the problem. Written documentation is also more likely to make teachers address administrative concerns more seriously and expeditiously. The form and procedures essentially encourage prompt, ongoing supervision and teacher responsiveness to that supervision.

III. Train Teachers and Supervisors To Collect Data

An essential part of this and all other supervision models is the collection of data supporting concerns recognized by supervisors and inspiring strategies for addressing those concerns. With this in mind, it becomes vital to provide some training for supervisors and teachers in data collection. Data collection methods fall into basically two categories: peripheral documentation and classroom observation documentation.

Peripheral documentation includes memos, letters, and official notices of any kind addressing problems that occur *outside* of the classroom. The memo in Exhibit 3-5, cited as documentation data in Exhibit 3-4, is an example of such official peripheral documentation. The theory is that, if an incident warrants supervisory concern, the teacher should be given official notice that this is the case. If the teacher in Exhibit 3-4 had never been told that tardiness was noted on specific dates and deemed unacceptable, the teacher would have been given no data bringing the problem to the fore and no opportunity to correct the situation. Notice and an opportunity to correct is the essence of legally prescribed remediation. Tardiness and improper dress are both remediable behaviors. The teacher might not have realized that five minutes represents unacceptable lateness and poses both physical and academic threats to the children involved. The supervisor's memo lists dates and degree of lateness supporting a marginal rating in this area but, more importantly, conveys concern that the teacher's lateness does affect safety and academic job expectations.

Records of parent complaints might be used in a similar way to support a marginal rating in the category of *rapport with parents,* whereas notes reminding a teacher that grades were late might be used to support marginal performance in the area of *administrative cooperation.* This documentation is intended to act not as a bludgeon but as a tool in the supervision process, a tool bringing problems to the attention of teachers and giving them timely incentives for working with supervisors to resolve issues of concern. The Trait Model itself is the instrument used to bring it all together, i.e., to gather repeated memos, notes, and complaints together to justify a rating showing concern with a given trait—a concern that must be addressed. Such documentation is used to draw the teacher's attention to the need for change and to make the Trait Model a viable supervisory instrument.

It should be noted, however, that documentation need not be *only* negative. Commendations for accomplishments can and should be used in the same way to justify superior ratings in a given area. Thus, letters from parents commending a teacher or from an administrator thanking a teacher for performance above and beyond that called for by contract are also valid data sources to support a system of positive reinforcement often overlooked in the process of teacher supervision. Everyone benefits from being substantively told that they are doing a good job, and teachers in this culture of criticism are particularly in need of positive reinforcement.

Classroom observation data, in contrast to *peripheral data,* are gathered in a variety of ways, depending on the focus of classroom supervision. Keith Acheson has provided an extensive set of approaches for objective data collection while observing classroom teaching, including *Selective Verbatim, Observational Records Based on Seating Charts, Wide-Lens Techniques* using video and audio recordings, and *Checklists and Timeline Coding of Teacher and Student Performance.*[10] Effective supervision requires a thorough repertoire of data collecting techniques, and each chapter of this text discusses ways to develop instruments to collect data addressing the specific supervisory situation and focus presented.

There is no single way to collect data. Ultimately, good classroom supervision requires that data collection be tailored to the perceived needs of the teacher being supervised. This usually means that the observing supervisor must pay more than one visit to the teacher's classroom or spend more than a passing moment observing teacher performance beyond the classroom. The initial classroom visit or attention-grabbing incident merely identifies perceived need (the gut feeling about what is right and what needs improvement). The follow-up visits or observations are used to gather data to substantiate perceived need (to validate the gut feeling or take it off the slate) and to clarify supervisory direction.

For example, if, on a first visit, the observer perceives that a teacher is not involving the children beyond the fourth row in instruction, the second visit would be used to gather seating chart documentation that this was, indeed, happening. With the seating chart data in hand, the supervisor can now bring to the conference suggestions for correcting this oversight. Seating chart data collection is a good starting point for analyzing *student involvement* and *teacher rapport* with students, two commonly cited traits. Seating chart data can also be used to address parental or student complaints of discrimination or pedagogical neglect. Supervisors using seating charts can identify students not participating in the lesson and can record teacher interaction with students in all parts of a classroom.

IV. Conferencing

Supervision conferences can take place before or after an observation is made. The need for a preconference has long been debated. A preconference does give the supervisor insight into the lesson's objective, the makeup of the class, and the sequence of learning and learning activities that may be evolving. Some, however, argue that a preconference using the Trait Model reduces the actual classroom observation to a show-and-tell event with little supervisory substance. Ultimately, the need for a preconference is determined by contract or supervisor choice.

In contrast, a postconference must always take place if supervision is to be effective. A postconference is the meeting between teacher and supervisor to discuss the pivotal supervisory event, in or out of classroom, creating the need for a postconference. For the Trait Model of supervision to be truly effective, the teacher should have received a copy of the data informing the supervision process before the postconference takes place. Reprimands, letters of commendation, classroom data collections—whatever has been the basis for the judgments rendered on the Trait Model forms—should be part of the information that a teacher receives prior to the supervisory postconference. For supervision to be effective, teachers will need time to analyze and interpret the data that the supervisor is using to support trait ratings. These data will be the focus of the postconference and should always be seen beforehand. Data preview allows a teacher time to digest the information, to explain, or simply to adjust to the need for improvement.

Ultimately, the goal of all supervision should be to give teachers the tools they need to monitor their own professional performances on a daily basis. With this in mind, it is wise to have teachers complete their own Trait Model supervisory forms, then to compare their perceptions of their performances, based on data gathered, with the perceptions of the supervisors. This advance activity will give the postconference focus.

Supervisors, for their part, should also take time to prepare for the postconference. This entails reviewing the data that they have shared with the teacher and deciding what they hope the conference will achieve. As teachers plan lessons, so should supervisors plan postconferences. They must isolate and prioritize the needs substantiated by their data collection. More importantly, they must be prepared with viable suggestions for techniques that will address these perceived needs. Simply telling a teacher that there is a problem is evaluation. Supervision entails helping the teacher to solve the problem.

There is also a human side to postconferencing. The supervisor must be alert to the personal dynamics that will come in to play, particularly during a remedial postconference. That is, it is vital that supervisors truly know the teachers they are conferencing with as individuals and attempt to work with the strengths of those teachers to achieve optimum results. Supervisors must never lose sight of the need to individualize supervision.

PROS AND CONS OF THE TRAIT MODEL

Done well, the Trait Model can have a significant impact on supervisory practice. It can use relatively simple forms and procedures to draw attention to and document real and perceived problems, and it can be a catalyst for meaningful discussion and change. The Trait Model, as a supervision tool, has the advantage of using a popular existing *evaluation* instrument in a genuine *supervisory* capacity by requiring that judgments rendered be supported by data and suggestions for improving performance. Its format is simple and direct, and, for teachers with few or no problems, it can also be an efficient and easy way to affirm a job well done to give the kind of positive feedback that is important but often overlooked.

Done poorly, i.e., without required orientation, documentation, or direction, the Trait Model is both an empty summative evaluation and an employment lawyer's dream. Without documentation, it becomes a totally subjective instrument open to dispute—a veritable grievance and lawsuit mine field. Done poorly, the Trait Model is also an easy escape hatch for weak and inept administrators who have the singular goal of avoiding potential mine fields and keeping their jobs at any cost. Unprepared with substantiating data or improvement plans, weak and inept supervisors will rarely make the critical judgments required to actually improve teacher and student performance. They will take the easy way out, never generating waves that they might drown in, but rather choosing to see every performance as "satisfactory" or "acceptable." Even when weak or inept supervisors do summon the courage to challenge "unsatisfactory" performance, without data to document their impressions, they will be forced to capitulate easily to any defense offered to the Trait Model judgments they've made, including a defense in the form of a demand for proof that the problem cited existed. Thus, the Trait Model used without supportive training, orientation, data collection, and notice can, indeed, become an instrument for maintaining mediocre and marginal teaching performance.

EVALUATING WITH THE TRAIT MODEL: A LEGAL PERSPECTIVE

Each of the models used to supervise can also be used to evaluate teacher performance, and there is a good argument for using the same instrument to both supervise and evaluate teacher performance. In that way, the same performance expectations are the focus of supervision efforts. However, when the Trait Model is used solely as an evaluation instrument, it leaves school districts and their administrators legally and pedagogically vulnerable in several respects. Failure to clarify expectations and means of data collection supporting judgments makes the Trait Model a legally challengeable assessment instrument, an instrument based on opinion and innuendo, rather than notice of expectations and concrete data documenting fulfillment of those expectations. Notice and evidence of performance are longstanding requirements in discipline or dismissal actions.

Another aspect of the Trait Model as an evaluation instrument open to legal challenge is the frequency of observation and data collection used as a basis for assigning a less-than-satisfactory performance rating. Reliance on a few observations of classroom teaching using a standardized instrument for counting discrete behaviors is a dubious basis for inferences about teacher competence.[11] Teachers challenging employment decisions that hinge on trait ratings will argue that only frequent observations supported by repeated unsatisfactory data should be used to infer negative performance. Legal remediation, as noted earlier, is becoming an expectation—not an option—in discipline and dismissal actions, and remediation is usually not achieved with a single silver bullet. Remediation is a process, not an event.

Even when remediation for questionable performance is not the question, notice and proof can also become issues in promotion and reward controversies. School districts, subject to collective bargaining agreements for every level of employee, must be prepared to justify their efforts to reward as well as their efforts to discipline or dismiss. Data supporting performance ratings take on new significance in deciding who gets a promotion, a merit pay raise, or a Career Ladder appointment. Administrators in the habit of giving all employees "satisfactory" performance ratings in every category to avoid controversy are likely to find themselves the center of controversy as they try to justify selecting one "satisfactory" employee over another for reward or promotion. In addition, although most promotion or reward disputes are settled through arbitration, some do make their way into the courtroom by virtue of discrimination or breach of liberty claims, discussed earlier. In either case, administrators hoping to have their decisions sustained will be required to justify those decisions by presenting real data verifying a difference in the degree of satisfactory performance reflected in a given trait.

THEORY INTO PRACTICE ACTIVITIES

1. In groups of five, isolate five characteristics or traits that all members of your group consider essential to the profile of a good teacher.

2. Decide on a rating scale to be used with each characteristic.
3. Develop a descriptive guide, illustrating each characteristic, how data will be collected, and how ratings will be assigned.
4. Use the instrument you developed in activities 1, 2, and 3 to actually observe and supervise a classroom teacher.
5. Discuss problems that you encountered in using your instrument.
6. How would you change the instrument or process that you developed?
7. Conduct a conference with the teacher observed, using your Trait Model Instrument, supportive data, and the descriptive guide that your group developed.
8. What kinds of data could you gather to substantiate a marginal performance in each of these trait areas found on supervisory instruments?
   - Teacher intellectual curiosity
   - Teacher mental and emotional stability
   - Teacher health and vigor
9. How would you provide remediation for these problems?
10. If your district uses a Trait Model, analyze the forms and procedures used, in light of the ideas discussed in this chapter.

NOTES

1. C.E. Finn, Jr., "The Real Teacher Crisis," *Education Week 29* October 1997, 48.
2. K.A. Acheson and M.D. Gall, *Techniques in the Clinical Supervision of Teachers*, 4th ed. (Reading, MA: Longman, 1997), 23.
3. The Educational Division of The Gallup Organization, *Teacher Perceiver Interview Guide* (Lincoln, NB: 1995).
4. Educational Testing Service, *The Praxis Series: Professional Assessments for Beginning Teachers* (Princeton, NJ: 1999).
5. G.L. Gordon, "Teacher Talent and Urban Schools," *Phi Delta Kappan 81*, no. 4 (1999): 304–306.
6. B. Marczely, "Teacher Evaluation: Research versus Practice," *Journal of Personnel Evaluation in Education 5* (1992): 279–290.
7. R. MacNaughton et al., "Effective Teacher Evaluation—Process Must Be Personalized, Individualized," *National Association of Secondary School Principals Bulletin 69* (1984): 1–11.
8. J.E. Morsh and E.W. Wilder, *Identifying the Effective Instructor: A Review of Qualitative Studies, 1900–1952 Research Bulletin No. AFPTRC-TR-54–44* (San Antonio, TX: USAF Personnel Training Research Center), 3.

9. E.M. Medley et al., *Measurement-Based Evaluation of Teacher Performance* (New York: Longman, 1984).

10. K.A. Acheson and M.D. Gall, *Techniques in the Clinical Supervision of Teachers* (New York: Longman, 1992).

11. S. Stodolosky, "Teacher Evaluation: The Limits of Looking," *Educational Researcher 9* (1984): 11–22.

4

The Teaching Process Model

- Bloom's Taxonomy

- Motivation

- Data Collection for the Teaching Process Model

- Teachers Most Likely To Benefit from this Model

- The Postconference: Sharing the Process and Data Collected with the Teacher

- Pros and Cons of the Teaching Process Model

- The Process Model: A Legal Perspective

- Theory into Practice Activities

The Teaching Process Model

Chris is a teacher new to the building, but not new to teaching. In Chris's interview, Chris presented a very creative, activity-oriented approach to teaching science. Now, two months into the school year, Chris's approach is the problem. Students have complained about being confused and not really understanding the concepts required by the curriculum. Parents, too, have voiced concerns about Chris's teaching style. Chris is a potentially good teacher who does not seem to know how to structure a lesson.

T he Teaching Process Model for supervision focuses not on a list of traits or predetermined characteristics of the ideal teacher, but rather on the *process of teaching* itself, as it occurs in the classroom. The supervisor in this scenario is interested in the way the lesson is planned, presented, and implemented. This model is based on research that has identified a pattern of instruction that is particularly effective in teaching new skills. Barak Rosenshine called this model *explicit teaching* because it defined effective teaching in terms of goals and steps that could be clearly described and analyzed.[1] Other researchers, most notably, Madeline Hunter, also analyzed the process of teaching, and it is significant that the models developed by Hunter and others draw similar conclusions concerning the steps present in effective classroom teaching. Exhibit 4-1 compares the steps in Rosenshine's *Explicit Teaching Model* with those in Hunter's *Instructional Theory into Practice Model*. In each case, the parts of the lesson identified parallel each other and identify similar basic formats for successful instruction. Terms may differ, but concepts are basically similar. Good lessons are planned and contain identifiable parts that are the building blocks of an effective presentation.

Although number and descriptive titles given to the steps may differ, basically, the Teaching Process Model is built on the assumption that all good lessons begin with review, in order to put learning in a

Exhibit 4–1 Comparison of Explicit Teaching Model and Instructional Theory into Practice

Rosenshine[2] *Explicit Teaching Model*	*Hunter*[3] *Instructional Theory into Practice*
1. Review	1. Anticipatory Set (review)
2. Presentation	2. Statement of Objectives
3. Guided Practice	3. Information Input
4. Correction and Feedback	4. Modeling
5. Independent Practice	5. Checking for Understanding
6. Weekly and Monthly Review	6. Guided and Independent Practice
	7. Closure

context, then proceed through presentation and modeling to activities structured to give students an opportunity for guided or independent practice in the skill taught. Time devoted to any one step will vary with the difficulty of the subject matter and the aptitude of the students involved.[4] However, in theory, all good lesson plans will contain all steps to one degree or another. Good lessons also show evidence of planning for such factors as motivation, retention and transfer, and the development of critical thinking skills. In summary, teaching is a process that can be codified and monitored.

BLOOM'S TAXONOMY

Those who focus supervision on the process of teaching examine the cognitive levels of questioning and learning activities inherent in each step of the teaching process, as well. Benjamin Bloom, in classic work, has identified six cognitive levels of learning, a virtual hierarchy of thought processing referred to here as *Bloom's Taxonomy*.[5] Exhibit 4–2 lists these cognitive levels of learning in descending order.

Knowledge, the simple assimilation of fact, is the lowest level of the taxonomy. *Comprehension* implies an understanding of what the factual knowledge means and how this new knowledge may be used, whereas *Application* is the actual ability to use learned information.

Exhibit 4-2 Cognitive Levels of Learning

Evaluation Synthesis Analysis	Higher Cognitive Skills
Application Comprehension Knowledge	Lower Cognitive Skills

Many lessons never get beyond these three basic steps in the learning process—these lower levels of cognitive thinking. *Analysis*, the ability to take information apart and examine it for deeper understanding, is the foundation for the development of higher cognitive skills. *Synthesis* is the ability to take facts that have been analyzed and restructure knowledge, to use known facts in new ways, and to form new ideas and uses for information that one has assimilated. Finally, *Evaluation*, the pinnacle of the taxonomy, occurs when the learner can compare and make value judgments regarding the facts and skills learned.

Bloom's Taxonomy is a hierarchy of cognitive skills but the taxonomy applies not only to levels of learning. In the context of supervising the process of teaching, the taxonomy also applies to the teaching that is taking place—the cognitive level of questioning and activities chosen by the teacher to help students develop these higher-order cognitive skills. As such, the taxonomy should be the format for teaching, as well as learning. Essentially, the taxonomy becomes an outline for improving the process of teaching with respect to cognitive development.

Satisfactory teaching never gets beyond the application level in the taxonomy. Superior teaching, however, must reach beyond these lower levels of cognitive skill development by structuring questions, activities, presentations, and tests that encourage higher-level student response and thinking. Superior teachers develop activities that require students to analyze, synthesize, and evaluate.

For example, consider the development of a lesson on making change for one dollar. The lesson may begin by having students identify the value of coins used in making change for one dollar (*knowledge*). The next step in teaching this lesson would be to have students purchase items at various prices less than one dollar and determine on paper what the change should be (*comprehension*). Step three in the process would be selecting the corresponding coinage to make the proper change (*application*). A lesson promoting analysis might have students determine at least two *other* coin combinations that would also make the proper change. For a *synthesis* activity, students might be asked to choose the combination involving the fewest coins and counting out the change. Finally, for *evaluation*, students might be asked to make other purchases under one dollar, each time making change with what they perceive to be the fewest coins. Alternatively, students could be asked to write short paragraphs explaining how they would determine what coins they would return to a customer making a specific purchase and why they chose one coin grouping over another.

It is easy to see that the second part of this simple lesson explores new cognitive skill territory. The level of thinking for the student is raised significantly, requiring reasoning and choice. However, the level of planning for the teacher must also be raised to achieve that higher level of learning. It will take planning, skill, and commitment for teachers to routinely develop lessons in all subject areas that go beyond mere application of learned fact. That is why the supervisor's attention must be focused on the *levels* of questioning, modeling, and independent practice that are part of the lesson, making Bloom's Taxonomy an integral part of Teaching Process supervision. Successful lessons should routinely expose students to all levels of the taxonomy.

Bloom's theory of learning levels is echoed in the work of Gagne, who believed there were eight kinds of learning, the lowest being "signal learning," in which the individual learns to make a general response to a signal, then many different responses to many different stimuli that resemble each other in physical appearance.[6] Gagne identified higher levels of learning as *concept learning, principle learning,* and *problem solving* and believed that learning was sequential, i.e., lower levels of learning in any given field must be mastered before higher levels can be mastered.

MOTIVATION

The ways in which teachers motivate students to learn is also an important part of this model's look at the process of teaching. Marginal and satisfactory teachers motivate with the threat of poor grades and detentions, i.e., they use negative incentives. Superior teachers are expected to bring a wide array of other learning strategies and more positive incentives into play to induce student involvement in learning. Some of the more significant and widely discussed strategies include those appearing in Exhibit 4-3. Ideally, superior teachers merge these motivational strategies in their classroom instruction.[7] When teachers don't use one or more of these strategies in the development of a lesson, the process often falters. Supervisors using the Teaching Process Model will be expected to know and call on these and other strategies in helping teachers to create superior learning opportunities that do motivate students.

Exhibit 4-3 Examples of Motivational Strategies

Strategy	Description
Wait Time	Teacher poses question and gives adequate time for response before calling on another student.
Learning Modalities	Lessons are planned to include an array of learning activities, including auditory, visual, tactile, gustatory, and olfactory.
Hemisphericity	Lesson activities are planned to address the needs of right-brained and left-brained learners.
Cooperative Learning	Students each play a part in completing a group learning activity.

DATA COLLECTION FOR THE TEACHING PROCESS MODEL

Because the process of teaching is the focal point of this model, supervisors will collect data emphasizing the structure of the lesson, the levels of Bloom's Taxonomy incorporated, and the motivational techniques employed. Madeline Hunter suggested that observers script tape lessons, i.e., that the observer make brief, objective notes on what is happening and what is said as the lesson progresses.[8] This written record then becomes the basis for Process Model supervision. The script tape can also contain time notations to show the time and order in which events occur and the amount of time devoted to each step—all factors pertinent to the process of effective supervision.

In analyzing the script tape of a lesson, the supervisor attempts to caption segments of the lesson that correspond to steps in the Teaching Process Model and to the levels of Bloom's Taxonomy. The presence or absence of a given step or factor will become the focus of the supervisory conference with the teacher. It should be emphasized, however, that there may be good reasons why a particular step or level was omitted in a lesson. Rosenshine elaborated on several of these reasons.

> It would be a mistake to say that this small-step approach applies to all students or all situations. It is most important for young learners, slow learners, and for all learners when the material is new, difficult, or hierarchical. In these situations, relatively short presentations are followed by student practice. However, when teaching older, brighter students, or when teaching in the middle of a unit, the steps are larger, that is, the presentations are longer, less time is spent in checking for understanding or in guided practice, and more independent practice can be done as homework because the students do not need as much help and supervision.[4(p. 62)]

The captioned steps become a guide in assisting the teacher to analyze and structure lessons that contemplate the unique needs of students and the special demands of the subject matter. The observer may also use script taping to point out the presence or absence of efforts to motivate students through the techniques noted in Exhibit 4–3.

In addition to scripting and captioning, supervisors might use the data collection technique known as *selective verbatim* to study the caliber of teacher questioning or student response observed with respect to Bloom's Taxonomy. Selective verbatim involves recording select parts of what teachers or students say during the lesson. If the observer wants to bring the level of questioning to the teacher's attention, the teacher's questions or student answers throughout the lesson would be the focus of data collection. Analysis of this form of data collection involves looking at the type of response that each question evokes and correlating that response with a level of cognitive achievement in Bloom's Taxonomy.

Because the way the teacher teaches is the focus of this model, audio- and videotaping, as well as scripting and selective verbatim, can provide a record of the process of teaching. Which means of data collection is chosen depends on the degree of teacher and administrator comfort with a method, as well as possible contract limitations. Many teachers do not feel comfortable having their performances taped, and many teachers' unions will defend a teacher's right to resist these more invasive methods of data collection. Ideally, the supervision process itself should be clearly designed to assist—not assess—thereby alleviating any threat from data collection in any form. If tapes of the lesson remain with the teacher after a supervisory *conference* discussing the data, the threat of technologic supervision should be removed, and teachers can begin to benefit from the technologic supermarket available to them. How data will be collected during a classroom observation and what will happen to the data are factors in any clearly delineated supervision process. An example using the Process Model to analyze a scripted lesson follows in Exhibit 4–4.

TEACHERS MOST LIKELY TO BENEFIT FROM THIS MODEL

Teachers who grapple with lesson development, organization, and successful implementation in the classroom, as did Chris in the opening scenario, are most likely to benefit from this approach to supervision. Veteran teachers who are already successful at what they do in the classroom would find assistance with structuring and lesson development an intrusive waste of their time. On the other hand, teachers who are new, inept, or inexperienced in classroom

Exhibit 4–4 Process Analysis of a Scripted Lesson

Teacher said that students would learn how to solve simple linear equations. → **Anticipatory Set/Objective**

Teacher put three linear equations on the board and proceeded to solve them. → **Presentation**

Teacher told students that the object of their numerical operations was to have x alone on one side of the equation.

Teacher said that, to do this, one must remove all other numbers by simple computation. → **Instructional Input**

Teacher used the equation $x + 5 = 25$.

Teacher asked how 5 could be deleted. Students responded by subtracting it away.

Teacher then said that to maintain the balance of the equation, what one did to one side, one must do to the other side.

Teacher illustrated by writing $x + 5 - 5 = 25 - 5$ on the board. → **Modeling**

Teacher then completed the computation, leaving $x = 20$ as the root of the equation.

Teacher then told students to use this same procedure to solve the equation $x + 57 = 139$. → **Check for Understanding**

Several students quickly yelled out the correct answer, $x = 82$. Others seemed confused.

The teacher moved on to the next problem, $x - 19 = 90$.

Again, several students yelled out the correct answer, $x = 109$, but others remained confused.

Next, teacher passed out a worksheet that students were to complete during the class.

Teacher circulated, checking students' individual progress and providing assistance where needed. → **Guided Practice**

Teacher distributed a sheet illustrating how the answers to the worksheet problems were found.

Teacher distributed another worksheet of equations to be solved for homework. → **Independent Practice**

Teacher summarized the process that students should use by solving one additional equation. → **Closure**

The bell rang and the students left.

teaching may need and welcome assistance in controlling the way that they use time to present new material and give students an opportunity to absorb and apply it.

Actually, teachers at any stage of their careers who fail to inform, motivate, or challenge students adequately would benefit from an observer's analysis of their attention to Bloom's Taxonomy and to the various techniques in Exhibit 4–3 that have proven successful in the process of motivating students. In short, teachers with reputations for marginal or mediocre performance will find this model helpful in creating lessons that inspire and challenge students to engage in higher-level thinking.

THE POSTCONFERENCE: SHARING THE PROCESS AND DATA COLLECTED WITH THE TEACHER

To truly profit from this model, the teacher must receive some preliminary training in both the theory and practice of the model. Teachers who are unfamiliar with the research on effective schools dealing with the steps in a well-planned lesson cannot be held accountable if those steps do not appear in their lessons. A brief overview of this supervision model, with an outline of the steps considered essential to a well-planned lesson, will give teachers a chance to practice planning and developing appropriate lessons. In addition, knowing the way that data will be collected and interpreted will reinforce the importance of the steps in the process, i.e., lesson structure, as well as the level of questioning, motivational techniques, and activity planning integral to this model's implementation. Thus, if a school adopts this approach to supervision, orientation and training in what is expected and how achievement will be measured is essential.

One of the prime advantages of this model of supervision is that it provides teachers and supervisors with a common vocabulary to describe and discuss what they see and do in the classroom. An orientation to this method of supervision is essentially a review of accepted and tested good teaching practice. Other professions have long ago acknowledged the need to share a common language and effective methodology, a professional context for developing good practice expectations and evaluating individual achievement. The Process Model does this for teachers, and schools that use this approach are much like teaching hospitals, where good professional practice is a shared focus.

In postconferences following supervisory observations, the steps of the Process Model should be used to focus attention on the structure of the lesson. A record of things said and done that correlate with the model's steps (see Exhibit 4–4) can be used to help the teacher to analyze the lesson for both form and substance. A record of questions asked or answers given by students will help the teacher to evaluate the level of questioning used. A record of learning activities will help the teacher to assess whether all learning modalities were addressed and whether attention to hemisphericity was part of the planning. In short, the postconference should give teacher and supervisor an opportunity to reflect on how the lesson was taught, in light of what educational research has found to work.

PROS AND CONS OF THE TEACHING PROCESS MODEL

The Teaching Process Model provides a blueprint for lesson development with which most teachers can agree and a common vocabulary for teachers to use in describing what they do. Moreover, the effectiveness of this step-by-step approach to teaching is supported by the research in the effective schools movement. It is a tested approach for improving teacher effectiveness in the classroom that has withstood the challenges of time. More recent research by Wang, Haertel, and Walberg[9] and by Good[10] reinforces the findings of these earlier studies regarding the most effective teaching strategies. The work of Joyce and Weil[11] also echoes some aspects of this earlier research. In addition, the work of Newmann and Wehlage,[12] dealing with Authentic Instruction, has enunciated five standards of higher-order thinking, depth of knowledge, connectedness to the world beyond the classroom, substantive conversation, and social support for student achievement that parallel Bloom's Taxonomy.

Another advantage to using this model is that, like the Trait Model, it eliminates the need for a preconference once teachers have been made familiar with the model's format and expectations, thus saving time in actual administration. Hunter contended that preconferencing is unnecessary and time-consuming, and that a well-trained observer should be able to collect all of the necessary information without a pre-observation meeting with the teacher.[13] Although some teachers and supervisors believe that preconferencing is always necessary to clarify any unique features of the class to be observed, allow for guided reflection, and relieve anxiety,[14] Process Model proponents would advocate discussing these features at the mentoring postconference. It can be argued that preconferencing, if done routinely and without specific need, can destroy the spontaneity essential to meaningful supervision. All classes, not just those earmarked for a supervisor's visit, should be well-planned and -implemented learning experiences. Announced observations can relegate observed lessons to mere "show-and-tell" rituals, in which alerted teachers can be sure that the supervisor will see all prescribed steps and procedures effectively implemented, *at least on the day the supervisor is present.* Such planned rubrics can prove a waste of time for both teacher and supervisor if they do not reflect what happens *every* day in the classroom.

Negative reviews of this model stem from the rigidity with which some supervisors may adopt and use it. There is concern that Rosenshine's cautionary statement regarding this model when it first appeared may be forgotten or ignored in application. Rosenshine cautions that lessons in which equal attention to all steps is not obvious will be deemed total failures. However, the model, like the process of supervision itself, is not intended to be a yardstick for simply measuring and "evaluating" teacher performance. The model, like the process of supervision, is intended to be a guide to assist teachers in improving their classroom performances. With this in mind, the postconference should discuss the reasons that not all process steps appeared and should evaluate the validity of the reasons offered. There may, indeed, be valid reasons for omitting one step or another on a given day, but if a teacher repeatedly ignores the need for anticipatory set, independent practice, or closure, model proponents maintain that the teaching process will ultimately not be as effective as it might. It should be a goal of the model to have the process act as an inner planning compass for teachers, a compass that makes them rightly uncomfortable when a lesson's plan is incomplete without valid justification.

Another criticism of this approach is that it supervises the teacher's performance *only* in the classroom. The model provides no way to assist teachers in improving their performances beyond the classroom. That is, this model does not address issues of rapport with parents, collegiality, administrative accountability, or compliance with work rules not relevant to the classroom performance. For example, this model provides no way to assist a teacher in conducting effective parent conferences or in grading in a timely and fair fashion. Unlike the Trait Model, its focus is, indeed, restricted to the teacher's classroom performance to the exclusion of all other aspects of a teacher's professional profile or responsibilities.

Still others are concerned with the availability of supervisors trained in a given discipline and question the ability of a supervisor untrained in a particular discipline to provide the guidance required by this model. How can one trained in the field of mathematics critique an English class? How can an observer trained in physical education assist a Spanish teacher?

Proponents of the model respond to these concerns by noting that the model focuses on the structure of an effective lesson, regardless of actual course content. They maintain that all good teaching is structured in the same essential way and that all good teachers plan for cognitive growth through questioning and learning activities spanning a range of learning modalities. Supervisors, proponents argue, can always render a judgment on the effectiveness of the process of teaching. Even when unfamiliar with the subject matter itself, the observer, as the students, can decide what is and what is not effective in the learning experience presented. Some would go so far as to say that supervisors unfamiliar with the subject matter presented are actually in an ideal position to render judgments regarding the effectiveness of the teaching process used because they, like the students, must learn subject matter totally new to them.

THE PROCESS MODEL: A LEGAL PERSPECTIVE

The Process Model is one of the best ways to address the need for remediation in classroom performance. As noted, it draws on established research to give specific guidelines to use in planning for instruction to teachers having trouble teaching. The legal requirements for notice and remediation are both addressed by this model. The courts have long held that teachers have no constitutional right to persist in a course of teaching behavior that contravenes an employing board of education's valid dictates regarding appropriate classroom methods or content.[15] Although teachers have some measure of freedom in teaching techniques employed, course content and coverage is manifestly a matter within a school board's discretion.[16] A board of education legally waives this discretionary right only when it fails to supervise or give prior notice regarding acceptable course content and methodology.[17] Thus, boards of education have both a right and a duty to supervise all elements of classroom instruction, and the Process Model provides a framework for doing both.

Supervisors using this model should gather data that would anticipate correlation with the steps or focal points in the process. Verbatim scripting, audiotaping, and videotaping are the best ways to capture the process that a teacher uses in teaching, and these records can then be used to analyze the lesson presented in light of the recommended steps in the process. Such objective data collection also removes the shadow of subjectivity from the process and can be used to dispel claims of discrimination or harassment that may be expected to arise as a challenge to supervision.

Used as described and with the purpose of helping teachers to improve instruction, the Process Model is a researched, legally safe and straightforward approach to supervision. The only possible obstacle to its implementation might be the teacher's contractual or personal objection to audio- or videotaping. If the difference between evaluation and supervision has not been clarified, teachers may fear that videotaped or audiotaped lessons will be used as evidence in disciplinary actions. This obstacle, however, can be overcome if, as part of the supervision process, the teacher is allowed to retain possession of the data collected.

THEORY INTO PRACTICE ACTIVITIES

1. Observe and script a lesson. Then, using either Rosenshine's or Hunter's steps, analyze the lesson's structure and content to determine if all recommended steps are present.
2. Based on first-hand experience in conducting the observation in Activity 1, discuss the need for a preconference in using this model. Is it necessary? Why or why not?
3. Observe a class and record all of the teacher's questions. Then analyze the questions with respect to Bloom's Taxonomy (i.e., determine which level of the taxonomy each question addresses).
4. Observe a lesson taught by a teacher with an exemplary reputation using this model. Are all steps present in one form or another?

5. Observe and record the motivational strategies that a teacher with an exemplary reputation uses.

6. Ask several teachers whether you may either videotape or audiotape their lessons and discuss the teachers' responses to your request to gather data in these ways.

7. Conduct a supervising conference with a teacher after using this model to evaluate the level of student responses with respect to Bloom's Taxonomy.

8. Observe a novice teacher and use this model to critique lesson structure, use of the taxonomy, and motivational strategies.

9. Observe a class outside your area of certification using the Process Model and comment on your effectiveness as a supervisor in this class.

10. What concerns do you personally have with the use of this model?

NOTES

1. B.V. Rosenshine, "Synthesis of Research on Explicit Teaching," *Educational Leadership 43*, no. 7 (1986): 60–68.

2. List adapted from Rosenshine, "Synthesis of Research on Explicit Teaching," 60–68.

3. M. Hunter, "Knowing, Teaching and Supervising," in *Using What We Know about Teaching*, ed. P.L. Hosford (Alexandria, VA: Association for Supervision and Curriculum Development, 1984), 169–192.

4. Rosenshine, "Synthesis of Research on Explicit Teaching," 62.

5. B.S. Bloom, *Taxonomy of Educational Objectives: The Classification of Educational Goals. Handbook 1: Cognitive Domain* (New York: Longman, 1956).

6. R.M. Gagne, *The Conditions of Learning* (New York: Holt, Rinehart and Winston, 1970).

7. T. Guskey, "Integrating Innovations," *Educational Leadership 47*, no.5 (1990): 11–15.

8. M. Hunter, "Script-Taping: An Essential Supervisory Tool," *Educational Leadership 41*, no. 3 (1983): 43.

9. M.C. Wang et al., "Toward a Knowledge Base for School Learning," *Review of Educational Research 63*, no. 3 (1993): 249–294.

10. T. Good, "Teaching Effects and Teacher Evaluation," in *Second Handbook of Research on Teacher Education*, ed. J. Sikula (New York: Macmillan Publishing USA, 1996), 617–655.

11. B. Joyce and M. Weil, *Models of Teaching*, 5th ed. (Needham Heights, MA: Allyn & Bacon, 1996).

12. F.M. Newmann and G.G. Wehlage, "Five Standards of Authentic Instruction," *Educational Leadership 50*, no. 4 (1993): 8–12.

13. M. Hunter, "Let's Eliminate the Pre-Observation Conference," *Educational Leadership 43*, no. 6 (1986): 69–70.

14. A.J. Reiman and L. Thies-Sprinthall, *Mentoring and Supervision for Teacher Development* (New York: Longman, 1997), 180.

15. *See* Ahern v. Board of Education of the School District of Grand Island, 456 F.2d 399 (8th Cir. 1972).

16. Millikin v. Board of Directors of Everett School District No. 2, 611 P.2d 414 (Wash. 1980).

17. *See, e.g.*, Webb v. Lake Mills Community School District, 344 F. Supp. 791 (N.D. Iowa 1972).

The Instructional Objectives Model

- Check for Understanding

- The Supervisor's Role

- The Preconference

- The Observation

- The Postconference

- Data Collection

- Sharing Data with the Teacher

- Teachers Most Likely To Benefit from this Model

- Pros and Cons of the Instructional Objectives Model

- The Instructional Objectives Model: A Legal Perspective

- States Linking Teacher and Student Performance

- Theory into Practice Activities

The Instructional Objectives Model

Terry's lesson plans are exemplary, and Terry appears to know the subject matter very well. Nevertheless, over half of Terry's students have repeatedly failed the state's proficiency exams. Terry structures each lesson following the Hunter process; however, students are not learning, despite what appear to be exemplary lesson plans.

Having all of the steps in the Process Model appear in a lesson plan is no guarantee that learning will take place. A well-organized, process-proficient teacher is not always effective. Within the context of the process, instructional objectives must be clearly defined and must address the specific needs of the students who are expected to attain those objectives. Sometimes, the needs of individual students can be subjugated to the process. When this happens, a teacher may be following the plan, but students, nevertheless, do not learn. In such a case, the Process Model will not adequately assist the teacher. Instead, instructional objectives will become the focus of supervision. The Instructional Objectives Model ties professional accountability directly to student performance. The central concern of the Instructional Objectives Model is student achievement of prescribed objectives. The model itself has two objectives: to determine the extent to which students achieve predetermined instructional objectives and to assist teachers in helping students reach these objectives if problems arise.[1] The theory giving rise to this approach is that the best measure of professional accountability is actual student learning. The only way that teaching can ever really be deemed effective is if students are learning the prescribed curriculum. If they are not, the teacher is simply not effective, no matter how well intentioned or structured the lessons are. Attention to a prescribed teaching format cannot be substituted for substantive student learning. This method reflects a shift in research focus dealing with educational pedagogy from means to ends,[2,3] a shift that was at the forefront of the present accountability movement.

Under the Instructional Objectives Model, a teacher's first task is to develop appropriate objectives for students, reflecting the district's curriculum. To do this, the teacher must understand the curriculum and know how to break the curriculum into learnable objectives, sequenced so that, ultimately, all curriculum goals will be met. The supervisor in the Instructional Objectives Model assists the teacher with this task by helping the teacher to identify the *learning* that will take place at each step, the *conditions* under which this learning will occur, the *specific student behavior* that will show that learning has taken place, and the *measurement* process that will monitor the degree of mastery of a given instructional objective. This model requires that teacher and supervisor consult and clearly determine each of these facets of the Instructional Objectives Model at a preconference. The preconference is a prerequisite—not an option—for this model's implementation.

This model also requires that the instructional objectives agreed to in the preconference be *behavioral,* that is, *observable* and *measurable*. Because teaching success will be linked to student achievement, it is essential that each of the four parts of the instructional objective be clearly defined, agreed upon, and described in behavioral terms that can be readily observed and measured by the teacher and supervisor. Developing the instructional objective in this way also helps the teacher to plan for the learning that will take place. When the learning must be defined in behavioral terms, it requires a teacher to isolate the precise information or skill that will be the focus of the lesson and to create conditions or learning activities that will allow the desired behavior to be learned, observed, and measured. The Instructional Objectives Model tolerates no fuzzy thinking or planning in the creation or attainment of objectives. It requires that a teacher put all expectations in behavioral terms. The conditions describe the behavior of the teacher in setting the stage for learning with equal precision. An example of such an instructional objective would be:

Given a reading selection containing ten metaphors and ten similes, students will circle all similes and underline all metaphors with 80% correctness.

LEARNING─────▶ *Distinguish metaphors from similes*

CONDITIONS─────▶ *Given a reading selection containing ten metaphors and ten similes*

BEHAVIOR─────▶ *Circle all similes and underline all metaphors*

MEASUREMENT─────▶ *80 percent correct*

In the example, the teacher would have prepared the *conditions* under which learning would take place—a reading selection containing the required number of metaphors and similes—and defined the *learning* focus—identifying the difference between metaphors and similes. The student *behavior* is stated in *observable* and *measurable* terms, so that the observer and teacher will be able to see and determine the degree to which each student has learned this concept, and the exact process for *measuring mastery* is also described.

Ambiguous objectives do not lend themselves to the precise behavioral definition required by this model, and teachers must practice developing appropriate instructional objectives. Examples of fuzzy, unacceptable behavioral objectives follow:

• The student will learn the difference between metaphors and similes.
• The student will know how to add single-digit numbers.
• The student will appreciate the value of classical music.

These objectives are unacceptable because they are unclear, and the behaviors they allude to cannot readily be observed and measured. Short of a lobotomy, there is no way to measure the "learning," "understanding," or "appreciation" that are the essence of these objectives. However, these objectives could be stated in observable and measurable terms if the model's format is followed, as in these examples:

• Given a reading selection containing ten metaphors and ten similes, students will circle all similes and underline all metaphors with 80 percent correctness.

- Following a demonstration on how to add integers from 1 through 9, students will correctly solve 9 of 10 problems in which they are asked to add integers from 1 through 9.
- After attending a performance of Swan Lake, students will write a paragraph discussing at least one positive effect that the performance had on them.

CHECK FOR UNDERSTANDING

To check your own understanding of this model's format, identify the learning, conditions, behavior, and measurement present in each instructional objective in the preceding section by circling and labeling the language describing each element of the instructional objective. Try to identify the learning, conditions, behavior, and measurement in the first examples given. Compare these instructional objectives with later examples stated in the observable and measurable terms of the model. Can you see why precise definition is a prerequisite for effective supervision?

This model is designed to help teachers determine precisely what they expect students to achieve in each class, what they as teachers must specifically do to produce this result, what the students must do to show that the objective has been reached, and what level of achievement will be considered acceptable before moving on to another objective.

The idea of writing instructional objectives for students is not new. Popham and Baker,[3] Mager,[4] and McNeil[5] were all early proponents of this model of supervision. What is new is the irrefutable importance that this supervision model has taken on in this era of educational accountability. At the heart of this model's implementation lies the call for data collection to attest to the attainment of predetermined educational objectives and to spur investigation of the factors that might have affected objectives attainment. Costa and Kallick[6] have reiterated the need for educators to collect data continually and reflect on them as a stimulus for further inquiry. More recent research has also emphasized the need to view the failure to attain stated objectives as a learning experience for both teacher and student. Wise teachers are urged to use the classroom assessment process as an instructional intervention to teach the lesson that failure is acceptable at first but that it cannot continue; improvement must follow.[7] Success is defined as continuous improvement in meeting objectives, and proficiency assessments look not only at the number of students failing, but also at the degree of improvement from one year to the next. Stiggins[7] argues that teachers should receive professional development in assessment literacy to help them use classroom assessment of instructional objectives effectively to inform their teaching.[8]

THE SUPERVISOR'S ROLE

The supervisor's role in this model is not merely to gather data assessing student achievement of the objective. Teachers can do this themselves. Rather, the supervisor serves as a coach in helping teachers to set instructional objectives in keeping with the district's curriculum and in establishing classroom conditions conducive to this incremental achievement of learning. The preconference held with the supervisor is the forum for discussing each aspect of the instructional objective set for a class to be observed. Through the observation and the ensuing postconference, the supervisor assists the teacher in determining what worked and what needs adjustment, based on parallel data collected to measure student achievement and student involvement in the lesson. The following questions outline the focus of the supervisor in each stage of this process:

THE PRECONFERENCE

- What pretesting has been done to determine student preparedness?
- Why was this objective chosen—where does it fit in the curriculum?
- What objectives preceded this objective, and what objectives will follow this objective?
- What do you want students to learn from this lesson?
- Under what conditions will the new learning be presented?
- What *observable* and *measurable* behavior will indicate that learning has taken place?
- How will learning achievement be measured?
- What data will indicate that learning has taken place?

THE OBSERVATION

- Was the learning presented at the appropriate level of difficulty?
- Under what conditions was the learning presented?
- Were all teacher behaviors relevant to the instructional objective?

- Were all activities relevant to attaining the instructional objective?
- How did the teacher check for understanding during the lesson?
- Did the teacher adjust the lesson to address varying student needs?
- Did all students attain the instructional objective set for them?
- What observable behavior indicated that the instructional objective was attained?
- Which students did not attain the instructional objective?
- What observable behavior indicated that the instructional objective was not attained?
- What adjustments in the lesson would increase the likelihood of achievement?

THE POSTCONFERENCE

- Did all students learn as the teacher expected they would?
- Why did those who did not succeed have trouble?
- Was the objective set too difficult for the students?
- Was the objective set too easy for the students?
- What conditions or activities could have been changed to enhance learning?
- What will be the next instructional objective for this class?
- How will this next objective relate to the objective taught today?
- What conditions and activities should the teacher use to ensure that this new learning takes place?

These questions, although not all-inclusive, outline some of the relevant concerns of a supervisor assisting a teacher at each stage of this model. Notice that, ultimately, all concerns center on student learning alone. Researchers advocating this model believe that instruction should be goal-referenced, rather then means-referenced.[3,9] That is, they don't really advocate a singular approach to teaching. There is no prescription for what a teacher should say or do in the classroom, as long as what a teacher does results in student achievement. Teacher competence under this model is defined as the teacher's ability to formulate instructional objectives and to design and execute instructional sequences that enable pupils to achieve these objectives.[10] This model will address teacher traits or the process of teaching only as they may incidentally affect the conditions of learning that, in turn, affect student achievement. Only if a teacher's traits can be shown to affect a student's ability to attain the instructional objective set will they become an issue. Only if the lesson's structure interferes or enhances achievement will it become a focus of this model. It is the job of the supervisor to be the teacher's eyes and ears in determining what works and what needs adjustment to ensure student achievement of set objectives.

District achievement tests and state proficiency exams are legislated versions of this model. However, in each of these cases, assessment—not assistance—is the goal. In contrast, the Instructional Objectives Supervision Model is intended to inform and assist the teacher in defining and achieving learning objectives. In the real world in which politics and education are all too frequently reluctant bedfellows, it is obvious that professional accountability using the Instructional Objectives Model may well be the wave of the future, as well as the present. Even now, school districts find themselves developing instructional programs tailored to the questions on proficiency exams in an effort to help teachers and students meet the instructional objectives set and tested by state and federal departments of education. The Instructional Objectives method of supervision fits well into the accountability movement in education. It essentially provides a rubric for monitoring student achievement and the teacher performance that influences it.

DATA COLLECTION

The principal source of data for this supervision model is the record of student achievement of stated objectives. However, observation of student achievement alone would be relatively useless, amounting to mere assessment, without supervisory assistance in adjusting objectives, behavior, conditions, and measurement. Effective supervision under this model requires that the observer connect student achievement to teacher performance so that teacher performance can be adjusted to ensure optimum student learning. What does the teacher do or not do that affects the end result? How do students respond to the conditions that the teacher establishes for learning? This supervision model is, in essence, a cause-and-effect experiment in pedagogy. To this end, a variety of data collection methods can be used, and observers can improvise as needed to gather relevant data.

Exhibit 5–1 lists several potential pedagogical problems relevant to the student performance measured by this model and the kinds of data that can be collected to make a teacher aware of the problems that may be affecting student performance. Needless to say, one observation is not enough to provide this information. A minimum of two classroom visits is needed to isolate causes and effects, and to gather the data required to inform and assist the teacher in attaining instructional objectives.

SHARING DATA WITH THE TEACHER

For the postconference, two types of data should be analyzed: *Student Achievement* and *Relevant Other Behavior*. If all students have satisfactorily achieved the objective set; the planning and execution that contributed to that success should obviously be acknowledged. If, however, the lesson's objective was not achieved or was not achieved by all, data should be collected to try to explain why the shortfall may have occurred. Sharing the data with the teacher

---

Exhibit 5–1 Tabulating Cause-and-Effect Relationships

Problem Description	Data Collection
The objective was too difficult and students did not have the background.	*Selective verbatim*—a record of student questions and comments showing confusion.
Not enough time was given to practice.	*Timed scripting*—to show time for student practice.
Teacher presentation was unclear.	*Selective verbatim*—record of what the teacher said.
Students were inattentive and disruptive.	*Anecdotal description*—to show what teacher was doing when students misbehaved.
Students at the back of the room do not achieve the objective.	*Verbal flow chart*—to show that the teacher did not involve students in the back of the room.

should not be done in a scolding or recriminatory way, but rather in a manner that informs and assists.

One approach that might be helpful in taking the sting out of a perceived problem is to give the teacher both sets of data before the postconference, simply noting that the additional behavioral data may help to explain the shortfall in performance. Rather than attempting to tell the teacher what the problem seems to be, wise supervisors realize that it will be much more beneficial in the long term to allow teachers to discover their own shortcomings with the assistance of the data gathered. It is difficult to see one's own shortcomings or to evaluate one's decisions from moment to moment while at the front of a classroom. Supervisors must remember that their purpose is not to threaten or humiliate teachers by using this model, but rather to be a second set of eyes, assisting teachers in analyzing how they can adjust what they do to enhance student achievement.

Once the data have been shared and analyzed, the next step in this process is to work with the teacher to adjust the instructional objective or lesson conditions in such a way that students will be able to achieve the stated objective. Each part of the objective must be reevaluated in light of the data gathered. Was the learning objective appropriate? How can the conditions be adjusted to promote success? Was the behavior expected too difficult or too easy? Was achievement properly measured? These are the issues that should direct the postconference.

TEACHERS MOST LIKELY TO BENEFIT FROM THIS MODEL

Teachers whose students are not achieving would benefit most from supervision using this model. State proficiency testing and district achievement testing will help to identify these teachers, but these are not the only ways to find teachers who might be helped with this approach. Parent dissatisfaction with student day-to-day progress or student complaints that the work in a particular class is either too easy or too difficult can also signal a need for professional accountability best served by the Instructional Objectives Model. If proper instructional objectives are being developed, students should be making even, ongoing progress through the curriculum and achieving satisfactorily on most assessment instruments.

PROS AND CONS OF THE INSTRUCTIONAL OBJECTIVES MODEL

This supervision model comports well with the call for greater professional accountability for student achievement. It focuses on student achievement and provides a way to study the connection between student achievement and teacher classroom performance. Because it is highly unlikely that public concern with student achievement will soon disappear, the major advantage of this supervision model is that, used properly, it provides assistance instead of blame. Ignoring poor performance is not an acceptable response to the call for professional accountability. This model does not ignore either disappointing student achievement or teacher performance that may be contributing to it. Instead, it offers ways to identify and correct that performance and consequent student achievement.

Proponents of this model maintain that instructional objectives serve as a virtual road map for all instruction. That is, instructional objectives clearly state the basic skills, facts, and concepts that a student is expected to master in order to have a useful understanding of a given subject. In a similar vein, the Instructional Objectives Model requires the teacher, working with the supervisor, to analyze and divide the curriculum into sequential, attainable learning objectives. To do this, the teacher must have a firm grasp of the curriculum and the subject matter encompassed. Educators with only a superficial understanding of the subject being taught will find it extremely difficult to do what this model requires.

Opponents counter this claim of subject matter proficiency by maintaining that this approach actually trivializes learning. Knowledge is broken into tiny manageable capsules, precluding a global view or any unanticipated learning or outcome. They maintain that this approach to supervision does not allow for deviation from the lesson plan or the creative sidetracks that have come to be known as *learning moments*. The Instructional Objectives Model is also the antithesis of constructivism, the theory that learners, not teachers, control their learning and that controlling what students learn is virtually impossible.[11] Constructivists argue that students must be permitted the freedom to think, to question, to reflect, and to interact with ideas, objects, and others—in other words, to construct meaning.[12]

Another often-cited weakness of this model is the potential for its emphasis on student achievement to cloud its value as an assistance model for teachers. Achievement and assessment are synonymous in the eyes of the model's critics. They feel that the assistive value of the model is outweighed by the threatening specter of student assessment as a factor in teacher assessment. With this in mind, teacher unions have resisted any effort to base the evaluation of teachers on student achievement, citing factors beyond the control of classroom teachers that may inhibit student learning.[13] In response to these objections, proponents of the Instructional Objectives Model have emphasized an absolute need to assign responsibility for achievement to those paid to accept it. If the task of educating today's children is beyond the ken of teachers, due to factors beyond their control, what is the purpose of public education and why are teachers paid to participate in a presumptively futile enterprise for which no one accepts responsibility? McNeil speaks for accountability proponents when he says:

> The failure to educate all students and the massive academic retardation which exists, especially among minority group students, has brought home the fact that one cannot judge a teacher as good solely because the teacher is following recommended procedures or meets categorical expectations. It is becoming essential to note the consequence of procedures and personal qualities upon learners: If the learners are not progressing as desired, the teacher has not been successful even if ascribed requirements are met.[14]

The Instructional Objectives Model provides the necessary link between student achievement and teacher performance that is missing in other, less strategic approaches to supervision and professional accountability.

Another criticism of the model is its emphasis on the predictability of learning, the notion that all learning can be described in terms of behavioral objectives with measurable outcomes.[15] Critics believe that reliance on measurable outcomes does not take into account the unanticipated learnings that are frequently significant outcomes of instruction and that rigorous compliance to an instructional objectives methodology stifles creative teaching and learning. Proponents of this model respond that "unanticipated" learnings are, indeed, unpredictable and that public education's funded purpose must not be left to chance. There should be some guarantees for the tax dollar spent in the classroom. There must be some assurance that each student will leave the public school with at least the basic fund of information needed to function effectively in a democracy. Thus, the popularity of the Instructional Objectives Model grows with the demand for performance accountability.

THE INSTRUCTIONAL OBJECTIVES MODEL: A LEGAL PERSPECTIVE

Forty-eight of the fifty states now have policies establishing standards, assessment, report cards, and consequences.[16] Several states use the attainment of the standards they set to reward, punish, or simply publicly acknowledge the performance of schools, principals, and teachers.

STATES LINKING TEACHER AND STUDENT PERFORMANCE

- TEXAS holds teachers accountable for how their schools perform. One-eighth of a teacher's yearly evaluation is based on the school's performance on state tests.
- TENNESSEE sends "teacher-effect reports" to every teacher in grades 4–8 and to every high school math teacher. The reports describe how much that teacher influenced his or her students' scores on statewide tests. Principals may not take the results into account for teacher evaluations but can use them to provide advice to the teacher on professional development.
- COLORADO now requires student performance to be considered for teacher evaluations, but local districts must decide what that means.
- MINNESOTA offers teachers monetary rewards for student performance. The state gives Advanced Placement teachers $25 for every student who scores a 3 or higher on an AP exam.[17]

The standards set by states must be rigorous, academic, written in plain language, and measurable.[18] The Instructional Objectives Supervision Model fits well into the context of this growing national initiative. Properly implemented, the model is a means to a legislated end, posing few legal problems. The potential for controversy arises, however, when the model is improperly used. Unless prescribed by state law or allowed by contract, this approach will remain purely a supervision model, not an evaluation plan. Careful and thorough preconferencing and postconferencing are the keys to avoiding legal disputes with the instructional objectives approach to supervision. Even though the model is not intended for use in evaluating the teacher, it does have the aura of evaluation, in that it ties teacher success to observable, measurable student success. Some teachers and teacher unions will inevitably find this approach to supervision threatening. Thus, it becomes incumbent on the parties using this model to clarify in the preconference their goal of supervision, not evaluation, and to define clearly each of the four parts of an instructional objective: *the learning, the conditions under which the learning is to take place, the behavior that will indicate that the learning has taken place, and the means for measuring the adequacy of learning.* Specificity focuses the work of both the teacher and the supervisor, and will make it easier for the supervisor to diagnose related problems and to provide the targeted assistance that a teacher may need to reach the objectives agreed upon in the preconference.

It goes without saying that a teacher's repeated failure to attain instructional objectives can and should also become the focus of teacher evaluation. When poor student performance does become the basis for discipline or dismissal, however, the Instructional Objectives Supervision Model's records of observation, data collection, and conferencing will document district efforts to identify the reasons for poor student performance and to provide the teacher with meaningful remediation.

THEORY INTO PRACTICE ACTIVITIES

1. Develop an instructional objective in your subject area, stating the *learning, conditions, behavior,* and *measurement,* and teach to that objective.
2. Evaluate student achievement after teaching this lesson.
3. Work with another teacher to set an Instructional Objective for a class you will observe. Observe and collect data measuring student success in attaining the objective.
4. In light of your experiences using this model in Activities 1–3, critique its effectiveness.

5. Do you favor using student achievement as a focal point in the supervision of teachers? Why or why not?

6. Thus far, you have studied three models for supervising teachers. List them in order of preference and discuss reasons for your sequencing.

7. Does your school district use student achievement as a factor in teacher evaluation?

8. Survey teachers in your district to determine whether they favor using student achievement as a factor in the assessment of their own performances. Why or why not?

9. Survey ten area districts to determine whether any use student achievement as a factor in the assessment of teachers.

10. How are doctors, lawyers, and accountants supervised? Discuss the reasons why the evaluation of teacher performance should differ from the evaluation of other professionals.

NOTES

1. J. Tracy and R. MacNaughton, *Assisting and Assessing Educational Personnel* (Needham Heights, MA: Allyn & Bacon, 1993), 62–69.

2. J.D. McNeil, *Toward Accountable Teachers* (New York: Holt, Rinehart, and Winston, 1971).

3. W.J. Popham and E.L. Baker, *Establishing Instructional Goals* (Englewood Cliffs, NJ: Prentice Hall, 1970).

4. R. Mager, *Preparing Instructional Objectives* (Palo Alto, CA: Fearn, 1962).

5. McNeil, *Toward Accountable Teachers*.

6. A. Costa and B. Kallick, *Assessment in the Learning Organization: Shifting the Paradigm* (Alexandria, VA: Association for Supervision and Curriculum Development, 1995).

7. R.J. Stiggins, "Assessment, Student Confidence, and School Success," *Phi Delta Kappan 81*, no. 3 (1999): 196.

8. Stiggins, "Assessment, Student Confidence, and School Success," 198.

9. Mager, *Preparing Instructional Objectives*.

10. McNeil, *Toward Accountable Teachers*, 31.

11. M.G. Brooks and J.G. Brooks, "The Courage To Be Constructivist," *Educational Leadership 57*, no. 3 (1999): 18–25.

12. Brooks and Brooks, "Courage To Be Constructivist," 24.

13. B. Marczely, "Teacher Evaluation: Research versus Practice," *Journal of Personnel Evaluation in Education 5* (1992): 279–290.

14. McNeil, *Toward Accountable Teachers*, 14–15.

15. E. Eisner, "An Artistic Approach to Supervision," in *Supervision of Teaching: Association for Supervision and Curriculum Development Yearbook*, ed. T. Sergiovanni (Alexandria, VA: Association for Supervision and Curriculum Development, 1982).

16. W.C. Bosher, Standards-Based Education Reform (Paper presented at the Education Law Association 45th Annual Conference, Chicago, IL, November 1999), 1.

17. A. Bradley, "Zeroing in on Teachers," *Education Week 11* January 1999, 46.

18. Bosher, Standards-Based Education Reform, 1.

6

The Teacher Performance Objectives Model

The Teacher Performance Objectives Model

Lee has been teaching reading for 15 years, and although Lee's classroom performance is good, Lee has difficulty relating to parents and colleagues. Lee avoids parent contact and refuses to serve on any of the school's standing committees. Lee is a loner who contributes little to the school's program outside of the classroom.

T he Instructional Objectives Model, the Teaching Process Model, and, in many respects, the Trait Model all focus primarily on the teacher's performance in the classroom. A teacher's job description and professional responsibilities, however, extend beyond the classroom. Teachers have administrative, public relations, organizational, and professional growth responsibilities that are also an inherent part of the job. In order for schools to run efficiently, these aspects of a teacher's job are also elements subject to professional accountability. Morris Cogan actually defined *clinical supervision* as that which focuses on ways of helping teachers to improve classroom performance and *general supervision* as all supervisory activities that occur outside of the classroom.[1] The Teacher Performance Objectives Model, as described in this chapter, can be used for supervising teacher performance required *outside* of the classroom, or responsibilities only peripherally affecting the classroom. The focus of the Performance Objectives Model is not a generalized set of traits, the teaching process, or student achievement. This model focuses on the responsibilities and objectives unique to a specific teacher's performance outside of the classroom.

This model's scope of professional accountability is defined by job description, contract, and local and state regulations, as well as by administrative expectations. The model will address a wide variety of concerns that develop outside the classroom but, nevertheless, have an impact on the school environment. It can be used for both remediation and growth goals in three areas: Public Relations, Administration and Organization, and Professional Development. Examples of the types of accountability issues addressed follow. The first set of examples deals with remedial problems, whereas the second set illustrates growth opportunities. That is, the first set of examples illustrates some of the more common problems that can develop in each area, and the second set illustrates the range of opportunities for personal development in each area that the model can offer.

REMEDIAL EXAMPLES

Public Relations

- Teacher has difficulty communicating with parents and/or staff.
- Teacher leaves promptly at the end of the school day and refuses to serve on school committees.
- Teacher does not contribute to building needs.
- Teacher writes inappropriate or unacceptable notes to students' parents.
- Teacher is perceived as disagreeable by staff and colleagues.

Administration/Organization

- Teacher does not turn grades or reports in on time.
- Teacher frequently does not attend or stay until the end of required faculty meetings.
- Teacher does not call in for a substitute when absent.
- Teacher does not follow rules in faculty handbook (i.e., drinks coffee in halls and classrooms).
- Teacher does not teach the prescribed curriculum.

Professional Development

- Teacher must renew license as prescribed by law.
- Teacher needs to update computer skills.
- Teacher needs new teaching strategies to address proficiency deficiencies.
- Teacher needs to develop a discipline plan.

- Teacher needs to update skills and knowledge base in area of certification.

Although these examples address remedial issues, this model can also serve as the vehicle for growth objectives in each area cited for teachers who exhibit no deficiencies but have skills and interests that could result in worthy school and personal improvement plans. Examples of such growth projects follow.

GROWTH OPPORTUNITIES

Public Relations

- Development of a school newsletter for staff and parents.
- Service on a school improvement project committee.
- Presentation of a staff development program for staff or parents.
- Responsibility for news releases on school activities.
- Responsibility for parent night programs throughout the school year.

Administration/Organization

- Supervision of an administrative function, such as school-wide testing.
- Acting as an administrative intern responsible for assigned administrative tasks.
- Leadership of a school improvement committee addressing an identified need.
- Supervision of a student teacher.
- Service as a mentor for teachers new to the building.

Professional Development

- Taking courses needed for an additional degree or certificate.
- Professional writing (i.e., publication of a textbook or curriculum in subject area).
- Presentations at national meetings.
- Service on national educational committees.
- Participation in state-level programs affecting education.

Given encouragement and support, teachers are capable of identifying their own goals for change and developing strategies to achieve these goals.[2] The Performance Objectives Model formalizes the identification of goals and objectives and the encouragement and support needed to attain them.

THE METHOD

This model is patterned on the *management by objectives* approach to supervision prevalent in business and industry, where managers set objectives for employees that are vital to the accomplishment of organizational goals. Redfern's[3] research transferred this concept to the field of education. Redfern believed that a performance objectives approach to supervision would let teachers know precisely what was expected of them in terms of performance and would assure that they be given the resources and support needed to achieve those objectives. Iwanicki[4] can be credited with integrating school improvement and staff development with the performance objectives approach to supervision, thus giving the model the potential for positive personal growth and school improvement, as well as remediation.

The steps that a supervisor must follow in using the Teacher Performance Objectives Model are outlined in Exhibit 6–1. Basically, the teacher must have a clear understanding of what is expected and why. That is, if the objective is remedial in nature, the teacher should understand the relationship of the objective to job description, contract, or published work rules. If, on the other hand, the objective is growth-oriented, the teacher should make clear the educational purpose of the objective selected in a plan for professional growth.

In either case, the teacher's objective must be stated in *observable* and *measurable* terms, and the *conditions* for achievement of the objective should be delineated, as well as the *evidence* that will indicate that the objective has been attained. Plans for monitoring progress and dates for completion should also be made part of the written performance objective. Essentially, the teacher performance objective should be as clearly explained as the instructional objective for students discussed in the previous chapter.

The major difference between the two models is that performance objectives set for teachers will be directly affected by such organizational factors as job descriptions, teacher contracts, handbooks, and board and state regulations, rather than curricular goals and objectives. The form and substance of professional accountability described by this model must comply with the prescriptive and pro-

Exhibit 6-1 Teacher Performance Objectives Model

Steps in the Teacher Performance Objectives Model I. Establish Performance Criteria Prepare a Job Description Distribute Contract Distribute Teacher Handbook Distribute Student Handbook Share All Pertinent Rules and Regulations
II. Develop Performance Objectives Preconference with Teacher Develop Measurable, Observable Objectives Explain in Detail How Objectives Will Be Achieved Identify Evidence that Objectives Have Been Achieved Establish Timeline for Achievement of Objectives
III. Monitor Progress Conference with Teacher Review Evidence of Progress Adjust Objectives or Conditions As Needed Provide Additional Support or Supervision Required
IV. Determine Level of Accomplishment Conference with Teacher Review Evidence of Accomplishment Determine Level of Accomplishment
V. Follow Up Conferences As Needed

scriptive mandates of these external influences. For example, a performance objective can require a teacher to attend after-school faculty meetings only if the contract requires such attendance. However, a performance objective *requiring* a teacher to write a school newsletter is unenforceable unless it is part of the teacher's job description or is agreed to by the teacher.

Proponents of this approach see the performance objective plan as a contract between the teacher and supervisor, clearly defining all elements of responsibility. If the teacher's objective is remedial in nature, this performance contract gives the teacher formal notice of what changes are required and timelines for showing improvement, and identifies the evidence that will be used to show that improvement has taken place. It should be noted that although the teacher may have input into remedial performance objectives plans, they can and should be administratively imposed if the need arises.

Several states actually require remediation and remedial periods for both tenured and nontenured teachers in need of help, and the extent of this remediation can range from "confer and consult" to the development of a formalized written plan.[5] Exhibit 6–1 outlines the steps in the development of such a plan.

If the teacher's objective deals with personal growth, the teacher will obviously have more input into all facets of the process. Ideally, in both instances, the performance objective should be mutually agreed upon by the teacher and the supervisor during the preconference at which it is developed. In both growth and remedial situations, the model's value lies in its ability to frame issues and to monitor progress. This approach forces the teacher and supervisor to be specific in their definition of the expectations or issues to be resolved.

Data Collection

Because this model deals with performance outside the classroom, the methods of data collection used for the Teaching Process Model and the Instructional Objectives Model would be inappropriate. Data collected to substantiate the completion of this model's objectives will vary from plan to plan. To illustrate the type of data collection that might be used, two example performance objective plans follow. One sets a remedial objective; the other a personal growth objective. In each case, the type of data to be collected and the conditions for collection are clearly defined.

Remedial Plan

Performance Objectives and Rationale

I will communicate more often with the parents of my students, because the principal has received complaints that I do not let parents know how my students are doing until report cards are issued. Parents feel it is then too late to be helpful.

Performance Objectives in Observable and Measurable Terms

I will call each student's parents at least once per academic quarter to discuss the student's academic and social progress in my class. If I am unable to contact a parent by phone, I will write the parent a brief note discussing the student's academic and social progress. These calls will be made in a timely fashion (i.e., with a view to giving parents time to react and help students).

Conditions

I will make one call each evening when parents are more likely to be available. Receipts for long distance charges will be submitted for reimbursement.

Measurement

A log recording all calls made; date, time, and subject of discussion will be kept. In addition, I will keep copies of letters sent. The number of complaints that the principal has received at the end of the quarter will decrease.

Personal Growth Plan

Performance Objectives and Rationale

I will work with staff to select a new reading series, because the texts and materials we are now using do not address proficiency test objectives.

Performance Objectives in Observable and Measurable Terms

I will contact vendors and secure sample series for review by staff. I will set up sample series in library for faculty review. I will prepare and disseminate an instrument for evaluating each series. I will tally results and have top vendors make presentations. I will schedule presentations and have staff vote on adoption. I will submit staff's recommendation with rationale to the Board for adoption.

Conditions

The administration will make meeting rooms available and will provide secretarial and custodial assistance as needed.

Measurement

A reading series recommended by the faculty will be presented to the Board for adoption before the end of the school year.

It should be noted that administrative assistance is part of each of these performance objective plans. The Performance Objectives Model requires a record of supervisory assistance in attaining both

remedial and growth objectives. Legally, this is particularly important when the plan is remedial. If disciplinary action may result because the teacher has failed to reach the remedial objective set, the
supervisor may be required to show that notice that a problem existed was given and that needed assistance in resolving the problem
was provided in a timely fashion. In Ohio, for example, if a district
decides to nonrenew a teacher's contract, the teacher must first be
given a written report of the evaluation leading to nonrenewal that
includes specific recommendations regarding any desired improvements and the means by which the teacher may obtain assistance in
making such improvements.[6] As a general rule, such statutorily mandated procedures must be strictly followed or the teacher will be entitled to reinstatement with back pay.[7]

Conferencing

As Exhibit 6–1 implies, pre-, post-, and midterm conferencing are
part of this model. There must be a preconference to set the objective, to agree on how performance will be observed and measured,
to determine the conditions for assisting in performance, and to decide how data will be collected and objective completion measured.
Midterm conferencing, although not absolutely required, is recommended to check on progress and to determine whether the plan
needs adjustment. Postconferencing, however, is integral to this
model. The postconference is a time to plan for further supervision
and to develop additional objectives as needed. This supervision
model, like the earlier models, relies on the accumulation and
analysis of objective data to serve as the basis for the model's plan.

Data Collection

The kinds of data that would support using the Performance Objectives Model for supervising a teacher will vary from teacher to
teacher and situation to situation. However, the data should describe
the problem addressed, particularly when the model will be used as
part of a remediation plan. Exhibit 6–2 correlates the types of data
and recognized problems that would suggest developing a performance objectives plan of remedial supervision.

Exhibit 6–2 Recognized Problems and Data

Problem	Data
Teacher doesn't come to announced faculty meetings.	Memos asking teacher to explain reason for absences.
Teacher doesn't communicate effectively with parents.	A record of parent complaints.
Teacher is frequently absent on Fridays and Mondays.	A correlated record of absences.

Exhibit 6–3 correlates the type of positive data that would support using the Performance Objectives Model as a professional growth plan for a teacher. As with every other model in this text, the teacher and supervisor should begin by looking at the classroom. Only when classroom performance is exemplary can professional growth plans focus on projects outside of the classroom. Teachers with instructional problems are better served by supervision plans based on the Trait, Process, or Instructional Objectives Models that center on the improvement of teacher performance within the classroom. However, when there are no concerns with classroom teaching, the Performance Objectives Model can become a vehicle for personal professional growth and/or school improvement.

Supervisors who wish to use the Performance Objectives Model as a professional growth plan for a teacher or a school improvement initiative would be wise to really get to know the teacher opting for this plan. A track record of success can be the supportive data needed. However, there is a first time for everything, and a teacher performing well in the classroom should not be shut out from using this model a a growth opportunity simply because this is the first time.

A cautionary note should be added about using this model. Growth does not always equate with success. Growth does always equate with learning, and this model gives a teacher the opportunity to set objectives and to develop plans for attaining those objectives. Even when plans don't work out as expected, the teacher will learn by analyzing the obstacles that thwarted the plan. Supervisors are

Exhibit 6–3 Objectives and Supporting Positive Data

Evaluations must show that the teacher has no problems in the classroom and students are learning as expected.	
Objective	*Data*
Seek additional certification in a different area.	Evidence of need for teachers in that area.
Write a new mathematics curriculum.	Evidence of need for curriculum and teacher experience.
Present an in-service on new developments in subject.	A paper and plan for presenting; record of presenting.

there to help as needed but should not discourage teachers from the experience of setting growth plans that go beyond classroom performance, even though the results are sometimes disappointing.

TEACHERS MOST LIKELY TO BENEFIT FROM THIS MODEL

Teachers with initiative and the need to achieve personal and professional objectives outside of their classrooms will find this model helpful. Individuals can best judge their own learning needs, and they will be most motivated when they select their own learning goals based on their personal assessment of their needs.[8] This model will allow motivated teachers the opportunity to grow professionally by undertaking new and different projects from those they encounter as classroom teachers. This approach gives experienced, successful teachers who do not need to strengthen their classroom performance other rewarding professional accountability options. To this end, in the last two decades, several researchers have seen the value in integrating the supervision process and the school's own improvement plans.[3,9,10]

Teachers in need of assistance in dealing with their responsibilities beyond the classroom, however, will also find this model helpful. For one thing, the process will clear up any misconceptions they might have regarding job descriptions, contracts, and work rules. As a remedial accountability instrument, this model requires that all chips be on the table and that perceived problems and issues be clearly defined and adequately discussed. The model also requires that specific assistance be discussed and described in the accountability plan. Too often, teachers, particularly those new to the profession, don't really know what's expected of them or how to go about asking for the help they might need. The Performance Objectives Model brings openness and clarity to the process of asking for and getting help. It also makes supervisors and administrators aware of their responsibility to assist teachers in trouble.

PROS AND CONS OF THE PERFORMANCE OBJECTIVES MODEL

The openness and clarity discussed in the previous section is a real plus in using this model. Used properly, the model can be the catalyst for collegiality between the supervisor and teacher. This is no hit or miss single visitation model. It sets the stage for repeated, meaningful discussion of professional responsibility and accountability. The model requires that teachers, even those addressing remedial issues, actively participate in the development of all parts of the performance objective. This means that teachers must give serious consideration to framing the objective in terms that they will find attainable, under acceptable conditions, and with measurable, observable results that they will find fair. Essentially, teachers in trouble have to confront and analyze their problems, and actively participate in developing a plan to solve those problems.

Another obvious plus from this model is that it can provide growth opportunities for successful teachers, rather than wasting their time with useless supervisory rubric. These growth opportunities, in turn, can be part of the district's or school's own growth plan (i.e., teachers can tailor their personal growth plans to school improvement). They can become part of the bigger picture, leaders and participants who bring school improvement plans to fruition.

The greatest drawback to this approach to supervision is that it takes time. Done properly, at least two, if not more, conferences are required. Also, the supervisor must be available on call as a resource provider. The time this entails will usually be substantial.

Another potential problem with the model in its remedial mode is the possibility of a lack of agreement between teacher and supervisor on the objective, conditions, or means of measuring achievement. In the best of all possible worlds, every planning preconference will end in agreement. In reality, however, a teacher needing remediation may feel defensive and threatened by this model's specificity. Should this be the case, peer mediation or union participation in the process may prove helpful. That is, a neutral third party may be used to help the supervisor and teacher iron out areas of controversy in a remedial plan.

THE PERFORMANCE OBJECTIVES MODEL: A LEGAL PERSPECTIVE

When the Performance Objectives Model is used as a remediation tool, it has the advantage of documenting both notice and assistance. It also provides a format for confronting and analyzing all factors that may be causing the problem addressed by the model. Thus, it is a legally sound approach to dealing with problem behavior outside of the classroom.

It must be remembered, however, that the model's focus is defined by contract, job descriptions, teacher handbooks, and administrative precedents. Supervisors cannot set remedial performance objectives for behaviors that are not required by contract or job description. A supervisor, for example, cannot insist that a teacher chaperone a school dance, if chaperoning school dances is not part of the teacher's job description or contractual obligation. The supervisor can *suggest* that occasional chaperoning would show that the teacher participates in the life of the school beyond the classroom door, but unless the teacher is compelled to do so by contract or job description, the teacher has the right to refuse to chaperone. Therefore, it is important for supervisors to read and understand the contract and to develop job descriptions and teacher handbooks that encompass all foreseeable responsibilities before hiring takes place. Although most job descriptions include the obligation to perform "all other duties that may be assigned," the vagueness of that provision invites a grievance, and few unions will decline the invitation to limit teacher responsibility.

Teacher handbooks are legal documents that can be used to define expected teacher and employer behavior,[11] but handbooks cannot be at odds with negotiated agreements. If they are, in most instances, contracts will prevail because contracts, where they exist, are legally binding agreements negotiated by both parties. Handbooks, on the other hand, are unilateral creations developed primarily by the administration without union input. Only if an issue is not covered by contract may it then become the province of the administration. Most negotiated agreements, in fact, have *management rights clauses,* which essentially say that any item not covered by the contract will be determined by the district's administration.

This brief perspective on collectively bargained rights emphasizes the importance of the contract. It also emphasizes the importance of understanding the interface between contract, employee handbooks, and job descriptions. Supervision cannot exceed negotiated authority, but handbooks and job descriptions can fill the gap between the negotiated agreement and job expectations where management rights clauses allow. Thus, it becomes important for administrators to develop handbooks and job descriptions that do just that.

THEORY INTO PRACTICE ACTIVITIES

1. Develop a performance objective for a teacher who does not participate in any of the school's after-school activities, even though required to do so by contract.
2. Develop a performance objective for yourself that would give you the opportunity to improve your school.
3. What kinds of data could you use to show that a teacher was not following the school's adopted disciplinary plan?
4. Develop a performance objective for a teacher with personal hygiene problems (i.e., personal cleanliness). Conduct a mock conference.
5. Develop a performance objective for a teacher who has been accused of harassing another teacher. Conduct a mock conference.
6. Work with a fellow teacher to develop a performance objective that will help raise the school's proficiency test scores.
7. Discuss and compare your experiences in developing performance objectives for Activities 5 and 6.
8. Describe the kinds of supervisory assistance (conditions) that you could provide to assist a teacher in attaining each of the following performance objectives:
   a. *Teacher needs to get to school on time.*
   b. *Teacher needs to dress more appropriately.*
   c. *Teacher needs to get along better with other teachers.*

d. Teacher does not turn in reports on time.
e. Teacher does not follow school's discipline plan.

NOTES

1. M. Cogan, *Clinical Supervision* (Boston, MA: Houghton Mifflin, 1973), 9.

2. B. Dillon-Peterson, "Trusting Teachers To Know What's Good for Them," in *Improving Teaching: 1986 ASCD Yearbook,* ed. K.K. Zumwalt (Alexandria, VA: Association for Supervision and Curriculum Development, 1986), 29–35.

3. G.B. Redfern, *Evaluating Teachers and Administrators: A Performance Objectives Approach* (Boulder, CO: Westview Press, 1980).

4. E.F. Iwanicki, "Teacher Evaluation for School Improvement," in *The New Handbook of Teacher Evaluation,* eds. Millman and Darling-Hammond (Newbury Park, CA: Sage Publications, 1990),158–171.

5. P.A. Zirkel, *The Law of Teacher Evaluation* (Bloomington, IA: Phi Delta Kappa Educational Foundation, 1996), 35.

6. *Ohio Revised Code* § 3319.111 (B).

7. *See* Naylor v. Cardinal Local School District Board of Education, 69 OS3d 162, 630 N.E.2d 725 (1994).

8. D. Sparks and S.F. Loucks-Horsley, *Five Models of Staff Development* (Oxford, OH: National Staff Development Council, 1990).

9. E.F. Iwanicki, "Contract Plans: A Professional Growth-Oriented Approach to Evaluating Teacher Performance," in *Handbook of Teacher Evaluation,* ed. J. Millman (Beverly Hills, CA: Sage Publications, 1990).

10. T.L. McGreal, *Successful Teacher Evaluation* (Alexandria, VA: Association for Supervision and Curriculum Development, 1983).

11. *See, e.g.,* Woolley v. Hoffmann-La Roche, Inc., 499 A.2d 515 (1985).

7

Peer Supervision

- The Method
  - Time, Coverage, and Costs
  - Preparing Peers To Supervise
  - Training Tools
  - The Art of Questioning
  - Assistance, Not Assessment
  - Peer Supervision Outside the Classroom

- Teachers Most Likely To Benefit from This Model

- Pros and Cons of Peer Supervision

- Peer Supervision: A Legal Perspective

- Theory into Practice Activities

Peer Supervision

Madison Elementary School is a rather small school. Members of the faculty know one another, and there is a spirit of cooperation and a shared concern for professionalism and achievement. Chandler is new to Madison and has not yet become attuned to the culture of the school. There are many things that Chandler could do better, both in and out of class.

P eer supervision is not new. Peer review has been successfully adopted by many professions outside of teaching.[1] In a recent study, it was found that when administrators alone provide supervision to more than 11 teachers, other administrative duties and services suffer.[2] At the same time, research has shown positive results with peer assistance.[3-5] With this in mind, the potential importance of peer supervision becomes obvious. Peer teachers, like administrators, have daily opportunities to be exposed to all aspects of each others' professional performances and to form data-based judgments regarding professional effectiveness.

Peer supervision, as presented by this model, includes but goes beyond mere observation and comment on classroom performance. Schools are, after all, academic communities. Therefore, the range of professional activity open to peer review should include all aspects of participation in that community. Peer supervision should address performance relating to the classroom, the school, the community, and the profession. This peer-implemented approach is designed to be formative and developmental. Formative, developmental supervision is a nonevaluative process between two equals.[6] In a formative supervisory relationship, a peer offers summative information to assist.[7] That is, peers critique each other for the purpose of improving performance.

Good schools are marked by a high degree of professional collegiality, and peer pressure can serve as a catalyst for improving performance. When a teacher is surrounded by other teachers who exemplify and expect the highest degree of professionalism, they, too, rise to the occasion. Peer assessments are powerful influences on teacher practices and attitudes.[8] No one knowingly wants to be perceived as the weak link in a professional organization.

The model outlined in this chapter does not limit participation as a peer supervisor to the best and the brightest, nor are the teachers supervised only those with the least experience or obvious problems. This model is based on the premise that every member of a professional community, veteran as well as novice, can provide valuable feedback to every other member of that community. Teachers themselves have emphasized that a regular exchange of roles was essential to successful peer coaching and have noted that, in situations where a person wanted to be only the observer but not the teacher, tension and conflict arose.[9]

Teachers observe each other and interact on a daily basis in many different ways. Like doctors, lawyers, and accountants, the professional performance of teachers does not take place in isolation. They are part of an interdependent professional service organization. As such, teachers are affected by the work of their colleagues and do have opinions regarding their effectiveness in that organization. Peer consultation is reported as shifting teachers away from a spirit of competitiveness toward true collaboration.[10] This model provides guidelines that would allow and encourage peers to supervise each other, both in and out of the classroom.

THE METHOD

Peer supervision of classroom performance is growing in popularity as educators realize the value of supervision by those most involved in the education enterprise. Good and Brophy have stressed the advantage of teacher study groups in which teachers have information and resources, and analyze teaching in a collegial setting.[11] In the past, peer supervision has usually assumed a one-on-one approach. However, this model is based on groups of teachers observing each other. In this version of the Peer Supervision Model, every teacher in a given school or subject area would observe, collect data, and comment on the classroom performance of at least five colleagues. Such collaborative supervision is premised on participation by equals in making instructional decisions resulting in a mutual plan of action.[12] Essentially, a professional study group is formed for the purpose of mutual supervision.

Under this plan, the teachers being observed will be observed more frequently and by four different peer supervisors. As a result, good practices and bad practices should become apparent more quickly. When two or three observers highlight the same positive or negative behaviors in their commentaries on a given teacher's classroom performance, it becomes far more difficult to ignore their presence and effect on performance. In addition to this obvious result, observers, by virtue of what they see and comment on, will become more alert to all aspects of their own classroom performance. The end result is the fact that peer supervision will help teachers to recognize that they are capable of contributing significantly to the overall improvement of instruction.[13]

Time, Coverage, and Costs

The classroom Peer Supervision Model described will probably raise implementation concerns. It requires some degree of class coverage and time for teachers to observe, analyze, and conference. In education, class coverage and time equate with money, so costs will also be raised as a potential drawback to effective implementation. However, time, costs, and coverage are not the obstacles that they appear to be. Essentially, each teacher in a supervision group is required to observe four colleagues, record data to support opinions formed, and postconference with the teacher observed, and they have a full school year in which to make these observations.

There are several inexpensive ways to achieve this goal. Probably the least expensive approach would be to have teachers within a supervision group occasionally team teach, combining groups to free each teacher in the group to observe and conference with other members of the group. Combined classes could center on coordinated interdisciplinary themes, projects, and/or testing.

Administrators, as part of their ongoing support for peer supervision, can also cover at least one class a day, thus freeing up at least one teacher a day to participate in peer supervision. Administrative coverage serves a dual purpose. First, it provides cost-free class coverage and support for peer supervisors. Second, it gets administrators back into classrooms, i.e., back where the action is. Often, administrators forget what being in the classroom is like. The clientele is constantly changing, as are the needs and pressures facing classroom teachers. Administrative return to classroom activities provides on-the-job professional development for administrators, as well as for the teachers they are relieving for peer supervision activities.

Finally, traditional substitute coverage can be used to free teachers for peer supervision. One substitute dedicated for this purpose can provide one period of coverage for five teachers on a given day. The cost of such dedicated substitute coverage can be part of a district's professional development budget allocation or it can be financed by a grant. The costs are relatively minimal, when compared with the benefits to be gleaned from peer supervision. In the end, it is a question of priorities. If, indeed, a district is serious about improving instruction, it will find the time and money needed for meaningful supervision. Peer supervision, done well, has a successful track record that merits the effort.

Preparing Peers To Supervise

Peer supervision should never be introduced without serious discussion and preparation for its implementation. Conflicts arise due to differing values or interpersonal communication and problems of a colleague judging a partner's work.[14] Some researchers maintain that peer supervision must be voluntary and that successful improvement efforts are teacher initiated.[15] In the final analysis, however, to have effective peer supervision in the classroom, five elements must be present:

1. There must be defined leadership.
2. Procedures must be clearly stated.
3. Peer supervisors must be trained.
4. Participation must be voluntary.
5. There must be ongoing administrative support for the program.[16]

Although administrative intervention will usually be needed to initiate a peer supervision program, peer supervision will not succeed if it is perceived as administratively controlled. To be successful, a peer supervision program must ultimately be run for and by teachers with administrative support.

It is also important to define the purpose and procedures of a peer supervision program so that no misunderstandings undermine its effectiveness. The most effective peer supervision programs are formalized and officially sanctioned by the school district.[17] The role of peer supervisors in collaborative settings is one of halting the spread of isolationism among teachers and of assisting teachers in establishing new ways of cooperating with coworkers.[18] Nevertheless, an effective peer supervision program must grapple with such administrative realities as collective bargaining, peer selection criteria, and program goals and evaluation. If collective bargaining indeed exists, peer supervision may be deemed a term and condition of employment that must be negotiated.

Questions about how peer supervisors will be chosen and how their observations will be recorded and used can be daunting. An example of just how controversial peer supervision can be was recently seen in San Diego. Administrative leadership in the San Diego Public Schools decided that peer coaches would be a pivotal part of a broad school improvement plan, but the details of the plan became the core of controversy between the district and the 8,000-member San Diego Education Association.[19] Peer coaching met with fierce opposition initially and led to a negotiation impasse on the issue. Union officials were quoted as saying that the plan was a top-down effort that shut teachers out of the planning. Union leaders also said they feared that teachers participating in the program would be viewed as evaluators and critics sent by the administration.

Program concerns cited by the San Diego Education Association were legitimate interests that could have been addressed in the program's planning stage by cooperatively defining the program's purpose and procedures. San Diego State University eventually helped to resolve many of the union's concerns by offering to oversee the design of a peer-coach certification program, granting independent certification as peer coaches to its graduates. The university's program will help to define the purpose and procedures of successful peer coaching and will create an independent credential authorizing trained teachers to be peer coaches. The university, a neutral third party removed from the administration, will provide a format for implementation and selection that has proven acceptable to the collective bargaining agent. San Diego's experience should serve as an example to other districts contemplating peer supervision programs.

The Holmes Group Report, *Tomorrow's Teachers*,[20] noted that teachers must instruct classes all day long, with little or no time for preparation, analysis, evaluation of their work, or opportunity to exchange intellectual ideas with colleagues.[20] Questions of time, training, and authority are always central to effective peer supervision programs. To succeed as a peer supervisor, teachers must have:

1. Skills to make effective decisions;
2. The ability to deal with conflict;
3. Communication skills that build trust; and
4. The ability to work with other group members.[21]

Initial training in these skills should be provided before the program begins and should continue throughout the peer supervision program because involvement in peer supervision will inevitably present peer supervisors with new and changing problems.[22]

Administrators who wish to implement a peer supervision program successfully have to resign themselves to a supportive but limited role in the process. Coverage, training, and timely program evaluation are part of what administrators will provide, but actual implementation and supervision will be the province of the teacher peer supervisors. One vital intrinsic way in which administrators support peer supervision is by believing in its value, i.e., trusting in the ability of teachers to contribute in a meaningful way to the improvement of instruction.

Training Tools

Training in the techniques of clinical supervision will help peer supervisors to make meaningful and objective classroom observations in which they collect actual data to support their perceptions of the teaching they observe. There must, however, first be some uniform understanding of what effective teaching entails before one can begin to critique what a teacher does. The Trait, Process, and Instructional Objectives Models discussed in earlier chapters can be used to define the parameters of effective instruction or to develop some composite definition of effective classroom performance. It is, however, vital that an approach be selected and that teachers understand and agree with its underlying philosophy.

Conferencing and relational skills are also an important part of effective peer supervision. There are many versions of peer supervision afloat. Some are more directive than others. That is, in some conferencing models, the observer/peer leads the discussion, linking data collected during the observation to suggestions for improving performance. An alternative conferencing style would have observers collaborate with teachers in analyzing data and drawing conclusions regarding its significance to instruction. In other conferencing models, the observer's role is totally nondirective, with the observer guiding teachers through questioning to discover for themselves where problems exist and to find for themselves ways to address these problems. In a stratified sample of 210 K-12 teachers, 30 percent preferred supervisors to work with them nondirectively, 67 percent preferred supervisors to work with them collaboratively, and only 3 percent preferred supervisors to work with them directively.[23]

Probably one of the least directive approaches to peer supervision is *cognitive coaching*. Peers using cognitive coaching act as mediators, rather than as fixers in the process of peer supervision.[24] Costa and Garmston cast peers in the roles of coaches who work with teachers in a trusting relationship to facilitate mutual learning and enhance growth.[25] Peer coaches help teachers to analyze the reasons for the decisions they make in the process of teaching by skillful questioning. Cognitive coaches don't give answers. Instead, they serve as questioning catalysts to reflective self-analysis.

Whichever approach is chosen, it becomes important for peer supervisors to be trained in all the nuances of effective communication. Communication is a matter of setting and body language, as well as word choice. There is an art to reporting data collected during observations and to questioning and conferencing in such a way that communication is not obscured by personal idiosyncrasies or perceived as biased or offensive. Effective peer supervisors must be trained to be alert to the details of effective communication: *location, setting, tone,* and *body language.*

Conferencing should take place in a comfortable, private setting in which assistance, rather than assessment, is the focus. An evaluator will sit opposite a teacher, with a desk or distance between them. Separation establishes lines of authority. A peer supervisor, to be effective, will sit next to the teacher, emphasizing collegial exchange as opposed to authoritative confrontation. Timing will also establish the tone of a conference. Administrative conferences are often harried and hurried. That is, administrators, pressed by schedule demands, tend to stress getting to the point quickly, even if it means sometimes being short with a teacher. Many administrators also entertain interruptions during an assessment conference. The message sent is that the cause of the interruption is more important than the conference being held. Interruptions inevitably bring a negative tone to a conference. Interruptions are the up-close-and-personal equivalent of "call waiting." Peer coaches must be trained to avoid these "administrative" mine fields. To conference effectively, peer coaches and supervisors must learn to allot time exclusively for conferencing and to spend more time asking questions than giving answers. Peer coaches and supervisors should never view conferencing as a ritualistic administrative chore. Conferencing is the very heart of the collegial exchange needed for effective supervision.

The Art of Questioning

Supervisors must be trained to ask *open*—not *closed*—questions. Closed questions are those that can be answered with a simple "yes" or "no," leaving the questioner with no place to go.

Example:

Did you think the class met the lesson's objective?

Teacher Answer: Yes.

A peer supervisor who didn't agree with the teacher would be left with no choice but to disagree, leading the conference to take a confrontational turn.

Open questions, on the other hand, require more than a single-word response. Open questions require the respondent to answer in sentences and require genuine reflection.

Example:

What evidence do you have that the lesson's objectives were met?

Teacher Answer: That requires a review of data.

In this case, the teacher must offer specific evidence that the objective set in the lesson was met. Did the students answer the majority of the questions asked, did they finish the project, pass the test, participate positively in the lesson's activities?

Assistance, Not Assessment

Each approach to peer supervision in the classroom has its own rubric and defines the role and authority of the peer supervisor in that context. To be effective, however, peer supervision in the classroom must never be confused with evaluation, either directly or peripherally. Peer supervision's goal is assistance, not assessment. If peer supervisors become evaluators, teachers unions and teachers are likely to object. Historically, teachers cannot simultaneously be colleagues and assessors.[26]

Peer Supervision Outside the Classroom

The Peer Supervision Model presented in this text also provides for peer supervision of performance outside of the classroom. Peer supervision outside of the classroom falls into three categories: *professional growth, interpersonal relations,* and *personal characteristics.* It is important to stress that, if a teacher receives an unsatisfactory rating in any of these categories, as with all other models, the rating should be based on data or evidence supporting the rating. It is also suggested that this aspect of peer supervision be conducted in conjunction with a teacher's self-assessment of performance in these areas. In some respects, this model can function as the Trait Model, discussed in an earlier chapter. The one significant difference between this model and the Trait Model is that the ratings in each category will be determined by each of four independent peers and will be based on the peers' perceptions of the rated teacher's performance in each category. Another significant difference between this model and the Trait Model is that the model will be shared with and remain with only the rated teacher. It can never be used by the district, even as proof of an attempt at remediation. The purpose of the model is to inform and assist, not evaluate and punish. Used effectively, it will open the lines of communication between teachers in a given school and will address the difficult "people" problems that can sap the camaraderie of a school.

The following form, Exhibit 7-1, provides a sample list of areas covering some of the nonclassroom concerns that can be explored. This list is in no way offered as a complete and exemplary instrument. The list is a starting point. Categories and items may be added or deleted as a given faculty and peer supervision group prioritizes its own needs and values. A scalar rating can be used, as discussed in

Exhibit 7-1 Nonclassroom Concerns

I. PROFESSIONAL GROWTH
Participation in professional training (i.e., workshops, courses, classes)
Response to suggestions for improvement
Participation in school/district improvement committees
Contribution to school programs outside of the classroom
Additional degrees, publications, certificates
Professional memberships
Participation in state or national committees
Leadership at the local, state, or national levels

II. INTERPERSONAL RELATIONSHIP
Respect for dignity and worth of others
Honesty
Consistency
Positive attitude
Genuine interest and concern for others
Loyalty to the mission of the school
Willingness to follow rules and procedures

III. PERSONAL CHARACTERISTICS
Appropriate dress
Appearance and grooming
Clear, well-modulated speech
Dependability
Tact and diplomacy
Tolerance for different views

Chapter 3, to indicate the perceived degree of performance in each area, based on data gathered, or a simple *satisfactory, unsatisfactory* rating can be assigned.

TEACHERS MOST LIKELY TO BENEFIT FROM THIS MODEL

All teachers can benefit from the opportunity to observe first-hand how other teachers function professionally. Professional isolation is one of the core problems in traditional education practice. Teachers are given relatively few planned opportunities actually to talk about what they do and their roles as professionals within and beyond the classroom. The model requires them to do so. Moreover, it requires them to recognize collegial perceptions of their professional performance within and beyond the classroom.

Education is also a field where small problems of a personal nature are allowed to go unnoticed, sometimes festering and destroying the morale of a school or district. The out-of-classroom supervision element of this model gives teachers the opportunity to cite and address the interpersonal concerns that have the power to destroy professional relationships and reputations.

PROS AND CONS OF PEER SUPERVISION

On the negative side of the ledger, the Peer Supervision Model can be a vehicle for disillusionment and dishonesty, if used improperly or without the full faith and support of the teachers and the administration. A case in point is the fate of peer supervision in the Rochester Public Schools. The revised 1987 Rochester contract, modeled on the Carnegie Forum on Education and the Economy, recommended peer assessment as part of the shared decision-making process adopted.[27] Ten years later, in 1997, teachers were candid in acknowledging that many of their colleagues were filling out the required forms without engaging in any real examination of practice.[28] In addition, Rochester administrators scoffed at the idea that self-assessment with a committee of one's "friends" could be genuine and felt that peers had no real authority to assess teachers.[29] The Rochester experience epitomizes what can go wrong on both sides of the fence in implementing peer supervision. Given all of the complaints, the most recent Rochester contract now provides the option for teachers to return to an annual administrative evaluation in place of peer review, beginning in the 1997–98 school year.[30]

On the positive side of the ledger, the candid exchange of opinions and perceptions supported by objective data is vital to any attempt at meaningful change in education. Peer supervision trains teachers and supports them in their efforts to study their craft and their professional relationships. Teachers do not perform in isolation. They interact daily with both students and colleagues, and these interactions become the fabric of their professional reputations. Honest, data-supported perception can provide important information to teachers at all stages of their careers.

PEER SUPERVISION: A LEGAL PERSPECTIVE

Legally, it is unwise to cast teachers in a position where they will be making decisions regarding the hiring, firing, or disciplining of colleagues based on classroom performance. Colleague assessment is not part of a teacher's job description, nor are they certified or paid to make these ultimate personnel decisions. A teacher faced with discipline as the result of an uncertified colleague's evaluation could legally challenge the colleague's ability to make judgments affecting employment.

In many states with collective bargaining laws, the roles of teachers and administrators are distinguished by the administrator's authority to hire, fire, and discipline, and administrators are excluded from collective bargaining units to avoid the conflict of interest entailed by this authority.[31] These statutes also preclude teachers from involvement in decisions to hire, fire, or discipline unless they are employed as administrators.[32] Therefore, it becomes very important to maintain a plan for assisting, not assessing, teacher performance within any peer supervision program.

Peer supervision plans are most effective when they are collectively bargained, with scope and focus cooperatively determined by the teacher union and the school administration. Collectively bargained plans are more likely to be spelled out clearly, and any problems that do arise with implementation can be resolved through the grievance process.

Another potential legal pitfall in the development of a peer supervision program deals with the dual issues of confidentiality and defamation. Teachers who participate in peer supervision should be warned that, to be effective, programs must offer the assurance of confidentiality. There will be problems documented. If there were no problems, there would be no need for supervision. Communications between peer supervisors and teachers are privileged communications. That is, supervisors are free to be frank and truthful about their perceptions of a teacher's performance when conferencing with the teacher because that is, after all, the purpose of peer supervision. However, that right to be frank and truthful about a teacher's observed performance does not extend to anyone but the teacher being supervised. To discuss a teacher's shortcomings with others is to defeat the purpose of peer supervision and perhaps even invite charges of defamation.

THEORY INTO PRACTICE ACTIVITIES

1. Form a peer supervision group with at least two other teachers and observe each other teaching. Collect data supporting your impression of each other's effectiveness.
2. Conference with an observed teacher using a *directive style* (i.e., based on your data, *tell* the teacher what you think can be done to improve instruction).
3. Conference with an observed teacher using a *collaborative style* (i.e., share your data with the teacher, then exchange ideas about what the data show and what can be done to improve instruction).
4. Conference with an observed teacher using a *nondirective style* (i.e., share the data that you've gathered with the teacher and prepare questions that will help the teacher to *discover* how to improve instruction).
5. Conduct a conference sitting behind a desk and another sitting next to the teacher, then discuss the differences between the two conferences.
6. Discuss the feasibility of peer supervision with two administrators and summarize their reactions to the prospect of using this model in their schools.
7. Using the list given or developing a list of your own, do an *out-of-classroom* supervision conference with another teacher.

Remember that all less-than-satisfactory ratings must be supported by factual data (i.e., recorded problems).

8. Have the teacher in Activity 7 repeat the process with you as the subject of out-of-classroom supervision. React to the process.

9. Poll teachers in your building concerning the feasibility of a peer supervision plan.

10. Can you see any problems with peer supervision, as presented in this model?

NOTES

1. A.E. Wise and L. Darling-Hammond, *Licensing Teachers: Design for the Teaching Profession* (Santa Monica, CA: The RAND Corporation, 1988).

2. Gwinnett County Pilot Teacher Evaluation Framework, Unpublished manuscript (Lawrenceville, GA: 1987).

3. S.S. Roper et al., "Collegial Evaluation of Classroom Teaching: Does It Work?" *Educational Research Quarterly*, Spring (1976): 56–66.

4. B. Joyce and B. Showers, *Student Achievement through Staff Development* (New York: Longman, 1988).

5. R.K. Hillkirk and J.F. Nolan, "A Focus on the Culture of Teaching: Instructional Leadership through Shared Ownership, Inquiry, and Reflective Coaching," *Journal of Staff Development* 12, no. 4 (1991): 42–47.

6. A.J. Reiman and L. Thies-Sprinthall, *Mentoring and Supervision for Teacher Development* (New York: Longman, 1998), 7.

7. Reiman and Thies-Sprinthall, *Mentoring and Supervision*, 7.

8. S. McCarthey and K.D. Peterson, "Peer Review of Materials for School Teacher Evaluation," *Journal of Personnel Evaluation in Education*, 1 (1987): 259–267.

9. K.A. Acheson and M.D. Gall, *Techniques in the Clinical Supervision of Teachers* (New York: Longman, 1997), 228.

10. Acheson and Gall, *Techniques in the Clinical Supervision of Teachers*, 228.

11. T. Good and J. Brophy, *Looking in Classrooms*, 4th ed. (New York: Harper & Row, 1987).

12. C.D. Glickman et al., *Supervision of Instruction: A Developmental Approach* (Boston, MA: Allyn & Bacon, 1995), 167.

13. R. Alfonso and L. Goldsberry, "Collegueship in Supervision," in *Supervision of Teaching*, ed. T.J. Sergiovanni (Alexandria, VA: Association for Supervision and Curriculum Development, 1982).

14. Acheson and Gall, *Techniques in the Clinical Supervision of Teachers*, 228.

15. V. Bang-Jensen, "The View from Next Door: A Look at Peer Supervision," in *Improving Teaching: 1986 ASCD Yearbook*, ed. K.K. Zumwalt (Alexandria, VA: Association for Supervision and Curriculum Development, 1986), 51–62.

16. S.J. Tracy and R. MacNaughton, *Assisting and Assessing Educational Personnel* (Boston, MA: Allyn & Bacon, 1993), 123.

17. Tracy and MacNaughton, *Assisting and Assessing Educational Personnel*, 123.

18. D.M. Beach and J. Reinhartz, *Supervision: Focus on Instruction* (New York: Harper & Row, 1989), 255.

19. B. Keller, "Peer Coaching Plan Approved in San Diego," *Education Week*, May 19, 1999, 3.

20. The Holmes Group, *Tomorrow's Teachers* (East Lansing, MI: The Holmes Group, 1986).

21. Beach and Reinhartz, *Supervision: Focus on Instruction*, 256.

22. P. Raney and P. Robbins, "Professional Growth and Support through Peer Coaching," *Educational Leadership 46*, no. 8 (1989): 35–38.

23. K. Ginkel, *Overview of Study that Investigated the Relationship of Teachers' Conceptual Levels and Preferences for Supervisory Approach* (Paper presented at the annual meeting of the American Educational Research Association, Montreal) April 1983.

24. A.L. Costa and R.J. Garmston, *Cognitive Coaching: A Foundation for Renaissance Schools* (Norwood, MA: Christopher-Gordon Publishers, 1994), 132.

25. Costa and Garmston, *Cognitive Coaching: A Foundation for Renaissance Schools*, 3.

26. Tracy and MacNaughton, *Assisting and Assessing Educational Personnel*, 123.

27. C.E. Murray et al., "Rochester's Reforms: The Right Prescription?" *Phi Delta Kappan 79*, no. 2 (October 1997): 148.

28. Murray et al., "Rochester's Reforms," 151.

29. Murray et al., "Rochester's Reforms," 151.

30. Murray et al., "Rochester's Reforms," 151.

31. *See, e.g., Ohio Revised Code* § 4117.01(F).

32. *See, e.g., Ohio Revised Code* § 4117.01(F)(4).

8

Client Supervision

- Methods for Determining Parent Perceptions
- Conferencing
- Phone Conference Dialogue
- A Word about Parental Involvement
- Parent Surveying
- Report Carding
- Student Supervision
- Student Surveys
- A Word of Caution Concerning Survey Use
- Teachers Who Would Benefit from Parent and Student Supervision
- Pros and Cons of Client Supervision
- Client Supervision: A Legal Perspective
- Theory into Practice Activities
- Appendix 8-A—Forms for Client Supervision

Client Supervision

Fran is a good teacher with high standards, but Fran is perceived as a mean teacher who gives too much homework and not enough help. Unfortunately, Fran is oblivious to public perception, maintaining that a small group of lazy students is responsible for this unflattering reputation. She maintains that she will not compromise her standards in response to complaints from a small group of malcontents.

T his model is based on the premise that teaching, as all other professions, has a dedicated client base whose feedback should be a central element in any supervision process. All other professions, to some extent, are supervised by their clients. Patients who find a doctor ineffective supervise by airing their complaints, filing malpractice suits, or simply finding another doctor. Lawyers who lose cases will also see their client lists shrink with their reputations for success. Even mechanics who fail to make cars run find themselves shunned by patrons who perceive their work ineffective. This is the essence of client supervision and is present in every part of the free market economy. Client supervision gives rise to competition, and competition ensures quality and progress in most fields.

Public school teachers do not technically function in a free market economy because their clients do not choose them or have the freedom to leave them at will, and teachers themselves do not compete for students in their classrooms. Nevertheless, teachers are subject to indirect forms of client supervision. Informal communication, such as students' comments to parents or parents' comments to other parents, may have as much or more of an effect on teachers' informal status as do formal measures, such as teachers' ratings on classroom process scales or measures of student achievement.[1] Every time a parent complains, opts for home schooling, changes schools, or votes down a levy subsidizing public education, or every time a student gets poor grades, stops attending, or fails to pass a state proficiency test, these educational clients are indirectly registering criticism of teacher performance. Parent complaints, political opposition to public education, and poor student performance are forms of very valid client supervision that provide vital information concerning client perception of public education.

Reality and perception need not always be the same, but perception takes on a life of its own that will inevitably color reality. Most of what parents know about the school they learn from their own children, and they over-generalize on the basis of that limited data.[2] Ignoring the perceptions of parents and students may well be the match inflaming the present campaign for vouchers as an alternative to public education. Vouchers would make teaching a profession, subject to the same free market economy as other professions. Vouchers would give all parents the right and ability to withdraw, as clients, from what they perceive to be ineffective schools and teachers; they may opt for educational programs they perceive to be more effective.

These arguments aside, however, there are very immediate, practical reasons for wanting to know how students and parents *perceive* teacher performance. Teaching is an "affective" skill. Teaching must be *affective* in order to be *effective*. Perception will directly influence the success that teachers have in the classroom. Teaching does not occur in a vacuum. Student, parent, and public perceptions all play parts in the process. Learning is intimately tied to the way that teachers relate, or are perceived to relate, to the students and parents they serve. Those who argue against involvement of parents forget that no other group of citizens exerts a stronger influence on public opinion and that only through a broad sense of favorable opinion can the school expect to make significant progress.[3]

A student who feels threatened or simply out of touch with a teacher is likely to have difficulty learning from that teacher. A student who is distracted by a teacher's personal mannerisms or affronted by a teacher's attempts at humor, may spend the class preoccupied with matters quite irrelevant to the subject at hand. Public school teachers and administrators need only reflect on their own academic careers to recall examples of teachers from whom they could not learn for one reason or another. The difference is that tuition-paying adults in university settings pick and choose the classes they take and the teachers who teach those classes; public school parents and students cannot.

Similarly, children whose parents find a teacher ineffective or offensive will not learn from that teacher. A good school-community relations program should encompass the concept of a partnership between the school and parents, which calls for the free and continuous exchange of information between parents and teachers and the involvement of parents in school affairs.[4] Home and school must be mutually supportive if learning is to take place. Parents who question either the quality or quantity of homework assigned will directly affect its completion. Parents who disagree with positions that they "think" teachers have taken in class will promote student dissent. Parents who feel their children are being harmed by the learning experience will do everything in their power to counter that attack, including undermining the credibility and value of the teacher they perceive as the enemy.

However, how does a teacher know when parent and student perceptions are obstacles to learning if the teacher never asks? Parents have too few opportunities to interact with schools in a positive, professional manner.[5] In public schools, parents and students cannot simply walk away from teachers they perceive to be disagreeable or ineffective. Instead, they are left to fight a very private war, one the parent and student may not win but one that the teacher assuredly will *never* win. Presently, public education does not readily accommodate requests for teacher changes. Thus, problems that seriously hamper learning are often allowed to fester, and learning is sabotaged.

This Client Supervision Model provides several practical approaches to monitoring both student and parent perceptions of teacher performance. However, teachers must begin by acknowledging and nurturing the same respect for parent and student perception as that accorded client perception in other professions. These clients do pay the bills that keep public education viable. They are real, albeit silent, partners in the educational enterprise, partners capable of undermining or supporting that enterprise, based on their personal stake in it and their perception of its effectiveness.

METHODS FOR DETERMINING PARENT PERCEPTIONS

This model presents three distinctly different approaches for gathering parental input: *Conferencing, surveying,* and *report carding.* Each method involves a different focus and different procedures, but all essentially monitor parental perception of teacher performance. All provide feedback that can be used by teachers to make adjustments in their own mannerisms, methods, and motivations. None of these methods need be part of any official or negotiated evaluation plan. They should, however, be a part of every teacher's unofficial personal supervision plan.

CONFERENCING

There is nothing particularly new about the idea of parent conferencing. In this model, however, conferencing by the individual teacher occurs more frequently, and the information gleaned from one conference is always used to inform needed change and to set the stage for the next conference. This technique requires the teacher to make communication with the parent an integral part of the teaching process on at least a quarterly basis. Although it is true that schools already provide parent conference nights, these usually occur only once or twice a year and not necessarily at the convenience of the parent. Parent conferences are large-scale group activities in which the opportunity for a significant exchange between parent and teacher is limited by time and scheduling constraints. Conferencing, as prescribed by the model, would occur on a more regular and convenient basis, although not necessarily always in person. Conferences would more likely be held by phone. They need not be long conversations but would essentially amount to an opportunity to personally update the parent on all aspects of a student's progress and to make the parent aware of any concerns the teacher might have. The conference would also give the parent an opportunity to voice any concerns the parent might have. There need not be a rigorous format for this exchange; however, the dialogue outlined below can be used as a prototype.

PHONE CONFERENCE DIALOGUE

Teacher: I'm just calling to touch base with you and let you know how ____ is doing in my class. As you probably noticed, _____'s most recent test and quiz scores are _____.

Parent: Response will let teacher know whether a parent is monitoring student activity. If not, monitoring should be encouraged and an update on student performance provided.

Teacher: As to _____'s behavior, I find that progress is being made in _____, but I am concerned about _____.

Parent: Parent response should be used as springboard to getting the parent involved in reinforcing progress and in helping teachers address concerns.

For most students, this conversation with a parent need not last more than five minutes, but it will give the teacher a chance to speak directly to the parent. This method serves two purposes: (1) it addresses individual concerns, and (2) it develops and maintains communication and good public relations with the parents of students. Parents and teachers are, indeed, partners in the educational process, yet each belies the other's willingness to get involved and effectively communicate. This method makes such blaming reproach less likely. It should also be mentioned that, in this day of answering machines, pagers, Call Waiting, Caller ID, and Call Return, the likelihood of hearing from parents by phone is very, very good. There is little likelihood that the effort will be a wasted one.

Those who argue that such intermittent conferencing is time-consuming and unnecessary should note that the amount of time given to resolving problems that develop because of a lack of communication in the course of a school year far exceeds the five minutes that a phone conference requires. Think about the number of hours lost to teaching and learning when a teacher is faced with a student who either cannot or will not learn. Think also of the number of hours lost to effective planning and preparation for classes when a teacher must meet with irate parents and administrators to clear up misunderstandings and misconceptions. The regular conferencing prescribed by this method can make such forced conferencing obsolete.

A WORD ABOUT PARENTAL INVOLVEMENT

Educators say that they want parents to be more involved in their children's schoolwork, but educators make opportunities for such involvement few and far between, at present. A yearly parent conference night, requests to assist with the annual bake sale, and one-way report carding do little to invite *meaningful* parent participation in the educational process. Parents who feel that they have no meaningful input will eventually withdraw from any participation in the process. Educators who exclude parents or demean the value of their opinions set public education up for failure and blame. If educators continue to insist that they have all the answers, they will be expected to also accept all of the responsibility and all of the blame for the system's failures, or "wrong answers." Parents who are not invited to help solve public education's problems will themselves become part of public education's problems. Time spent becoming acquainted with parents and familiar with the student's home environment is vital; it is public education's version of business research and development.

PARENT SURVEYING

This method of securing parent input involves *group* rather than *individual* contact. The purpose of this approach is essentially to poll the entire group of parents served to get an indication of how the teacher's work is perceived by the group served. Much like a political poll, parent polling will give a teacher a glimpse of trends in parental opinion. If 30 parents are asked whether homework assigned is *too much, too little,* or *just right,* and 20 respond that they find it too much, there is a telling message in this number of responses. No matter what a teacher's own intent or perception may be, in this case, the amount of homework is probably too much. A teacher is likely to dismiss student complaints as self-serving, but when 30 parents attest to the time and effort consumed in completing assignments, it should give the teacher reason to pause and reconsider. Those teachers who would counter by declaring that parents have no right to determine how or what they teach should be reminded that parents do have both the right and the responsibility to protect their children from perceived harm, including the harm caused by educational failure and disillusionment with a system that is unresponsive to their concerns.

This chapter includes an *Appendix of Forms for Supervision* that gives several examples of parent surveys that could be used. Ideally, the instrument developed should measure reaction to all aspects of the teacher's classroom performance and should also give some space for free response (i.e., unstructured comments that may not have been addressed in the survey). The following issues should guide development of the surveys used:

- The Relevance of Work Presented
- The Quality of Teacher Presentations
- Teacher Attention to Individual Student
- Fairness in Evaluation and Grading
- Relevance, Quality, and Quantity of Assignments
- Perception of Communication with Parent

The surveys in the appendix have been developed by reviewing survey items actually used in some districts, but they are not necessarily right for all districts or all teachers. They have been included as examples to engender thought and discussion about the items that appear and the format in which they appear.

Teachers who use the survey format must resign themselves to the fact that surveys are most informative when they are returned anonymously. The need to identify them can inhibit the parental frankness that is needed. Also, surveys mailed home directly to parents with stamped and self-addressed return envelopes will be more likely to be returned with true "parent" input than those sent home with an "interested student." In the long run, the time and effort will be well worth it.

REPORT CARDING

Report carding is a method that attaches itself to the official report card sent home with the student. It is a written invitation to respond to the student's officially reported progress or lack thereof, in writing or by phone. Provision may also be made for a parent simply to note that the report card has been seen and that present efforts and practices should continue, as shown in Exhibit 8–1.

Exhibit 8–1 Sample Report Card Form

Dear Parent,

Please review your child's report card accompanying this note, then respond to the questions that follow or request an opportunity to discuss this report card in a telephone conference. Sign the bottom of this note and return it by mail to the address below as soon as possible.

1. Do you feel this report card is a fair appraisal of your child's progress?
2. If not, please use the space below to outline your concerns briefly.
3. What suggestions can you offer for improving your child's performance?
4. Check here if you believe that procedures in place should continue: _____
5. Check here if you wish to have a telephone conference with your child's teacher: _____

Parent Signature _____ Date: _____

Student: Chris Smith   Grade 10
9415 Maple Street   Mapleview High School
Any Town, Ohio 44321   33 Maple Street
Phone: 330-555-3892   Any Town, Ohio 44321

In contrast to the parent survey, the report carding procedure is *not* anonymous, nor does it cover as wide a range of questions or concerns. It should be addressed to the parent receiving the report card and may even be part of the report card itself—a signed comment card to be returned with or without the report card itself. Computer-generated report cards make the development of easily returned forms very easy. Nevertheless, there must also be a follow-up effort by the teacher to contact parents who do not respond.

If, indeed, parent involvement is important and teachers truly want parents to help them help children succeed, they must take the necessary steps to really involve them in the educational process. If teachers believe that parent input is important, parents will believe it, and they will become involved participants, rather than critical observers of the educational process. We all inevitably make time for what we consider to be important.

STUDENT SUPERVISION

The most fundamental form of student supervision occurs on a daily basis in every classroom. Student behavior, attendance, and achievement are all ways in which students indirectly critique and supervise teacher performance. Students resist inept teachers and become discipline problems.[6] A growing number of states are actually requiring consideration of student performance in the evaluation of teachers,[7] and no state prohibits use of student test results as part of a performance-based dismissal by statute or regulation.[8] If an entire class or large numbers of students misbehave or fail to achieve, the problem engendering such poor performance is unlikely to rest entirely with the students. Contrary to public perception, *not everyone can teach*. In fact, there are many adults who should never return to a classroom as anything other than students. Classroom control and the ability to engage students actively in the learning process are skills that many aspire to but not all achieve. When misbehavior or low achievement is a central problem, the adult in charge must be held accountable.

Student attendance is yet another parameter for measuring actual teacher effectiveness. There is something to be said for the philosophy that if one is doing what is expected and needed, *"they will come."* The classroom experience must be comfortable, reasonably attractive, and purposeful (i.e., students must see a point to their showing up on a daily basis, a point other than a misplaced masochism). Classrooms that are physically or emotionally abusive give rise to poor attendance, as do classrooms that are nonproductive and boring. Students can watch videos, read, and play at home. When they do these things in a classroom, teachers must prove that there is a valid educational purpose to the exercise. *Teaching, contrary to some popular opinion, is not a substitute for day care.* Teaching has a unique, publicly subsidized purpose that can be achieved only by creative, thoughtful, and professional educational planning. The ultimate question that teachers must answer for every exercise, activity, and assignment is, What is the learning? If such learning-centered planning does not occur, students are unlikely to come, particularly as they mature and begin to evaluate their other time use options. There is an enticing, exciting world outside of the classroom that competes with the classroom and the teacher on a daily basis.

Student response (i.e., achievement) is the final parameter for supervising teacher effectiveness. In the Instructional Objectives Model, the teacher sets the objective, conditions, and means for measuring achievement of the objective. In the Student Supervision Model, the objectives, conditions, and measurement of achievement are controlled by teacher, district, and state, but the student controls the element of behavior. Student supervision, through achievement or failure, occurs *every time* a student takes an exam or completes a project, or competes academically with peers.

District achievement tests and state proficiency tests will monitor student proficiency in attaining objectives not necessarily set by the teacher, but nevertheless deemed pertinent and important by state and national goals, and the means of measuring this achievement will be outside of teacher control. Courts, however, have consistently allowed use of student test scores to justify teacher nonrenewal and termination.[9] In the final analysis, students must learn if the job of teacher is to have any real relevance or security.

STUDENT SURVEYS

This method of supervision parallels that outlined for parents. Essentially, students are surveyed on a regular basis to determine their perceptions of their own progress and to identify areas in which the process of instruction can be improved. Early research on teacher effectiveness relied on student perceptions. In 1896, Kratz, in a study entitled "Characteristics of the Best Teachers as Recognized by Children," drew attention to the importance of student input regarding teacher effectiveness.[10] As with parental surveying, this process must begin with teacher respect and appreciation for student perception and opinion if the model is to have value. Evidence continues to suggest that students can make reliable questionnaire responses about classroom instruction.[11] Students of all ages have opinions regarding teacher performance. Therefore, students at all ages should be polled to monitor that opinion. As with parent surveys, these opinion polls can be used to identify opinion trends within a class, as well as to identify individual students in a group experiencing distinct conflicts and serious problems.

The appendix at the end of this chapter provides examples of instruments for surveying student opinion from kindergarten through high school. Once again, there is no intent to declare these forms particularly noteworthy or exemplary. They are simply examples of forms that can be developed to secure student opinion at various grade levels on pertinent classroom issues.

A WORD OF CAUTION CONCERNING SURVEY USE

Both parent and student surveys can be vital sources of information for a classroom teacher. However, they are rarely used because teachers fear how they will be interpreted and applied administratively. The possibility that parent and student surveys may become part of a teacher's official evaluation has led many teachers to avoid using them. Teacher unions cite the unpredictability of such polling as a concern. Teachers also point to parent and student lack of training in educational methodology as a reason to invalidate parent and student opinion concerning what goes on in the classroom. However, on a daily basis, we all render opinions concerning the work that others perform for us in a wide range of fields in which we ourselves are not trained. Few teachers are trained mechanics. Nevertheless, if, after having a car serviced, the teacher perceives that it is still not running properly, the teacher will register an opinion. That opinion may be registered through verbal or written complaint, and, if not addressed, that opinion will be registered by a change in patronage.

The question of how parent and student surveying will fit into the process of formal accountability is one that must be resolved through collective bargaining. Surveying need not be a part of the formal procedures adopted by a district, but it should be a method for measuring personal accountability used regularly by teachers themselves. The consummate professional wants public input regarding the service rendered. It is the way that a professional stays in business. A new system for evaluating principals in Charlotte-Mecklenburg, North Carolina, awards points for effectiveness in using both parent and student surveys.[12]

TEACHERS WHO WOULD BENEFIT FROM PARENT AND STUDENT SUPERVISION

Actually, all teachers would benefit from this supervisory approach. As stated earlier, teaching does not occur in a vacuum. There is a client audience in education that cannot and should not be ignored. Without client input, any profession can fail to evaluate its own effectiveness objectively. At present, the parameters and means for client supervision of teacher effectiveness exist but remain politically unpopular within a profession that still enjoys a controlling monopoly. The push to adopt vouchers threatens that monopoly and makes client input increasingly important to the survival of public schools.

PROS AND CONS OF CLIENT SUPERVISION

This model is a vital step in the development of effective public relations between schools and the communities they serve. Parents and teachers need to communicate but, at present, they do not effectively do so on any regular basis. Students and teachers must also communicate, but that fear, distrust, and professional inertia, too, often impede communication. This model opens new ground. It gives the teacher several personal, viable ways of resolving the problem of knowing what parents and students are thinking and ways of making parent and student input relevant to the delivery of educational services. This model makes education a true service profession.

If properly implemented, this model also provides not simply information, but rather a unique vehicle for promoting public relations. It publicly recognizes the importance of parents and students in the process of public education. Far too often, the teacher's and system's own interests obscure their roles. There is a pronounced tendency to dismiss the role of parent and student in public education because, ultimately, they are perceived as having no control over their status as clients. Parents may not agree with what schools and teachers do, but they have been relatively powerless to force either schools or teachers to change. To date, public school parents cannot pick and choose either schools or teachers without leaving public education. Public schools, however, do not exist simply to employ teachers. The primary purpose of public education is to provide a service subsidized by public funding, and education, as any publicly funded enterprise, has a need to evaluate the effectiveness of its efforts in the eyes of those providing that funding.

Teachers who value parent and student input become more like other professions, in that they recognize their dependence on public perception and their debt to those they serve. When this happens, teaching will become more of a free market enterprise, responsive to public opinion and stronger for that responsiveness. Perhaps teaching will at last acquire professional status in the eyes of a public that must itself cope with the changing perceptions of a free market.

On the negative side of the ledger lies the potential for bruised professional egos. The truth about how a teacher is perceived can, indeed, sometimes be disconcerting. Nevertheless, the need to know cannot and should not be sacrificed to the fear of knowing. Like an undetected cancer, negative parent and student perceptions can ultimately destroy the learning process, as well as the teacher's professional reputation. There really are no other negatives to this approach to supervision if, indeed, parent and student feedback remains with the teacher. It is a valid, relatively easy, and worthwhile procedure that can truly enlighten practice.

CLIENT SUPERVISION: A LEGAL PERSPECTIVE

In *Tinker v. Des Moines Independent Community School District*,[13] the Supreme Court declared that students do not shed their constitutional rights to freedom of speech or expression at the schoolhouse gate; it goes without saying that neither do their parents or guardians. The right to voice an opinion on matters of public concern in a manner that is not disruptive to the educational process has always been constitutionally guaranteed. However, the opportunity to voice an opinion on the way that the educational process personally affects them is rarely afforded to parents and students. The Client Supervision Model merely provides a constructive forum for parents and students to exercise their constitutional right to comment on their perceptions of the classroom experience.

The sample forms in Appendix 8A are presented as examples of forms for surveying parents and students. They are offered to engender discussion of items and format, with a view to personalized revision. It should be noted that many of the items appearing on the surveys address similar issues using slightly different phrasing. This is done to check on the validity of responses to similar issues. For example, in Sample Parent Survey Form I, items 11 and 17 both address the issue of perceived teacher fairness.

THEORY INTO PRACTICE ACTIVITIES

1. Discuss your own experiences in soliciting parent and student feedback concerning the quality of your work as a teacher.
2. Analyze the results of your students' latest proficiency or achievement tests. What do their scores say about your teaching?
3. Try calling your parents to update them on their children's progress. Do this at a time when no official conferencing is planned. What kinds of reactions did you receive for your effort?
4. Develop a one-page form for surveying student opinion regarding your teaching techniques and overall performance.
5. Administer your survey to your class and analyze survey results. Were they what you would have expected?
6. Develop a one-page form for surveying parent opinion regarding your teaching techniques and overall performance.
7. Send your survey home and tally the results. Were they what you would have expected?
8. Try the *report carding* method for soliciting parent response to each student's report card. Evaluate the effectiveness of this method of parental supervision.
9. What does your school or district do to find out how parents perceive the programs offered?
10. What does your school or district do to find out how students perceive the programs offered?

NOTES

1. T.L. Good and C. Mulryan, "Teacher Ratings: A Call for Teacher Control and Self-Evaluation," *The New Handbook of Teacher Evaluation*, eds. J. Millman and L. Darling-Hammond (Newbury Park, CA: Sage Publications, 1990), 203.
2. F.C. Lunenburg and A.C. Ornstein. *Educational Administration: Concepts and Practices* (Belmont, CA: Wadsworth Publishing Co., 1996), 192.

3. D.R. Gallagher et al., *The School and Community Relations* (Needham Heights, MA: Allyn & Bacon, 1997), 124.

4. Gallagher et al., *The School and Community Relations*, 123

5. Lunenberg and Ornstein, *Educational Administration: Concepts and Practices*, 193.

6. K.A. Strike, "The Ethics of Educational Evaluation," *The New Handbook of Teacher Evaluation*, eds. J. Millman and L. Darling-Hammond (Newbury Park, CA: Sage Publications, 1990), 369.

7. P.A. Zirkle, *The Law of Teacher Evaluation* (Bloomington, IA: The Phi Delta Kappan Educational Foundation, 1996), 31, 32.

8. Zirkle, *The Law of Teacher Evaluation*, 31, 32.

9. Scheelhasse v. Woodbury Central School District, 488 F.2d 237 (8th Cir. 1973), *cert. denied*, 417 U.S. 969 (1974); *In re* Termination of Johnson, 451 N.W.2d 343 (Minn. Ct. App. 1990); Johnson v. Francis Howell R-3 Board of Education, 868 S.W.2d 191 (Mo. Ct. App. 1994).

10. H.E. Kratz, "Characteristics of the Best Teachers as Recognized by Children," *Pedagogical Seminary 3*, (1896), 413–418.

11. R. Manatt, *Student Feedback to Teachers Questionnaire* (Ames, IA: College of Education, Iowa State University, 1987).

12. J.A. Murphy and S. Pimentel, "Grading Principals: Administrator Evaluations Come of Age," *Phi Delta Kappan 78*, no. 1 (1996): 74–81.

13. Tinker v. Des Moines Independent Community School District, 393 U.S. 503 (1969).

Appendix

8
A

Forms for Client Supervision

Exhibit 8A-1 Sample Parent Survey Form—I

Please circle yes or no in response to each of the following statements.

1. The teacher seems to know my child's strengths and weaknesses. Y N

2. The teacher effectively communicates with me. Y N

3. The teacher often gives my child work that is too easy. Y N

4. The teacher often gives my child work that is too hard. Y N

5. The teacher gives my child the right amount of homework. Y N

6. My child likes to go to school. Y N

7. My child likes the teacher. Y N

8. My child is sometimes afraid of the teacher. Y N

9. My child is afraid to ask questions. Y N

10. My child complains about school. Y N

11. My child says the teacher is unfair. Y N

12. My child enjoys classroom activities and talks about them. Y N

13. My child feels a part of the class. Y N

14. I have a fairly accurate idea about how my child is doing. Y N

15. I rely on the report card to let me know how my child is doing. Y N

16. I have met with my child's teacher at least once this year. Y N

17. I feel that my child is treated fairly in this class. Y N

18. I feel that I can talk to my child's teacher about issues I have. Y N

19. I know my child's objectives for the last marking period. Y N

20. I believe that my child's teacher has good classroom control. Y N

Exhibit 8A–2 Sample Parent Survey Form—II

Please circle yes or no in response to each of the following statements.

1. The teacher knows my child's abilities and interests. Y N

2. The teacher has kept me informed concerning my child's progress and problems. Y N

3. The homework assigned is too hard for my child. Y N

4. The homework assigned is too easy for my child. Y N

5. The homework assigned is appropriate for my child. Y N

6. The teacher encourages my child. Y N

7. The teacher's grading is fair and equitable. Y N

8. My child feels that the teacher talks too much. Y N

9. My child feels that the teacher has control of the class. Y N

10. My child complains that other students disrupt the class. Y N

11. My child complains about being treated unfairly in class. Y N

12. The teacher has talked to me about my child. Y N

13. I feel at ease in talking with my child's teacher. Y N

14. I feel that my child is making age-appropriate progress. Y N

15. My child finds school interesting this year. Y N

16. My child needs extra help in achieving goals set. Y N

17. My child likes and respects the teacher. Y N

18. My child feels comfortable in this classroom. Y N

19. My child's assignments are relevant and meaningful. Y N

20. I believe that my child's teacher is doing a good job. Y N

Exhibit 8A–3 Sample Student Survey—Grades 9–12

Please circle yes or no in response to each of the following statements.

1. I know the objectives for each lesson. Y N

2. My teacher gives reasonable assignments. Y N

3. My teacher listens to what I have to say. Y N

4. My teacher anwers my questions. Y N

5. I understand the work in this classroom. Y N

6. When I get things wrong, I eventually understand why. Y N

7. I have time to complete the work assigned in this class. Y N

8. I feel comfortable in this class. Y N

9. I am encouraged to think in the class. Y N

10. The work in this class is too easy. Y N

11. The work in this class is too hard. Y N

12. This class is managed well. Y N

13. Too much time is wasted in this class. Y N

14. The teacher respects me. Y N

15. The teacher likes me. Y N

16. I respect this teacher. Y N

17. I am treated fairly in this class. Y N

18. I find myself easily distracted in this class. Y N

19. This class bores me. Y N

20. The activities in this class are well planned and intersting. Y N

Exhibit 8A–4 Sample Student Survey Form—Grades 7–12

Please circle yes or no in response to each of the following questions.

1. Do you feel that the amount of work in this course was fair? Y N

2. Does the teacher help you when you have difficulty? Y N

3. Is the teacher open to questions from the class? Y N

4. Does the teacher respect your ideas? Y N

5. Is the teacher impartial and fair? Y N

6. Does the teacher tell you when you performed well? Y N

7. Does the teacher have a sense of humor? Y N

8. Is this class interesting? Y N

9. Is student discipline a problem in this class? Y N

10. Does the teacher lecture too much? Y N

11. Is there too much homework? Y N

12. Do you learn to think independently in this class? Y N

13. Is this class well planned and organized? Y N

14. Are you graded fairly in this class? Y N

15. Do you feel free to participate in this class? Y N

16. Can you use what you've learned in this class? Y N

17. Does the teacher respect your ideas? Y N

18. Do you like this class? Y N

19. Is the classroom atmosphere comfortable? Y N

20. Are you learning in this class? Y N

Exhibit 8A–5 Sample Student Survey Form—Grades 4, 5, and 6

Please circle yes or no in response to each of the following statements.

1. My teacher listens to what I have to say. Y N

2. My teacher tells me when my work is good. Y N

3. My teacher gives interesting homework. Y N

4. My teacher gives too much homework. Y N

5. My teacher likes some children better than me. Y N

6. My teacher grades me fairly. Y N

7. I'm afraid to tell my teacher when I don't understand. Y N

8. My teacher understands me. Y N

9. My teacher gives me work that is too easy. Y N

10. My teacher scares me. Y N

11. I know what my teacher expects me to do. Y N

12. My teacher is often too busy to help me. Y N

13. My teacher gives me work that is too hard. Y N

14. My teacher likes me. Y N

15. I like my teacher. Y N

Exhibit 8A–6 Sample Student Survey Form—Kindergarten through Grade 3

Show how you feel by circling a happy, so-so, or sad face as each question is read to you.

1. How do you feel about school? ☺ ☺ ☹

2. How do you feel when you are in school? ☺ ☺ ☹

3. How does the teacher make you feel? ☺ ☺ ☹

4. How do you feel about reading time? ☺ ☺ ☹

5. How do you feel about recess? ☺ ☺ ☹

6. How do the boys and girls in class make you feel? ☺ ☺ ☹

7. How do you feel about math? ☺ ☺ ☹

8. How do you feel about the activities in the class? ☺ ☺ ☹

9. How do you feel about the homework assigned? ☺ ☺ ☹

10. How do you feel about what you do in the class? ☺ ☺ ☹

9

Self-Supervision: The Professional Portfolio Model

- Portfolio Self-Supervision: Model

- The Method
  –Data Collection
  –Conferencing

- Teachers Most Likely To Benefit from This Model

- Pros and Cons of Portfolio Self-Supervision

- Portfolio Self-Supervision: A Legal Perspective

- Theory into Practice Activities

Self-Supervision: The Professional Portfolio Model

Kim has taught for 20 years and has been recognized as an exemplary teacher on both state and local levels. Kim is a mentor teacher admired by staff, students, and parents—a mature, exemplary professional in every sense of the word.

PORTFOLIO SELF-SUPERVISION: MODEL

S elf-supervision through the development of a professional portfolio is a relatively new approach to teacher professional accountability. Historically, self-assessment has been considered of little value—a strategy of self-improvement fraught with problems.[1] In the past, self-supervision was limited to classroom performance, and many teachers perceive their performances as very different from reality. However, it was critical in self-assessment that teachers become aware of their actual teaching behavior.[2] Carroll[3] listed five major methods for conducting self-supervision: self-rating forms, self-reports, self-study materials, observation of colleagues' teaching, and videotape/audiotape feedback. At best, however, most self-supervision plans had teachers using the same trait model instrument that administrators would use to evaluate their performance in order to compare their own perceptions with those of the administrator. Until recently, professional performance beyond the classroom played no significant role in self-supervision. Fortunately, more recent models for self-supervision have expanded the field for supervision, giving teachers a broader range of activities to include in their assessment of professional performance.

One such model, Performance Appraisal Review for Teachers (PART), provides opportunities for teachers to design and complete their own annual assessment procedures, including traditional administrative observation and evaluation.[4] Assessment in this model might also include a portfolio of the teacher's work, peer review of teaching, or a collaborative effort with other teachers.[5] A portfolio is a purposeful collection of work that records one's learnings, dispositions, development, and demonstrated teaching ability.[6]

These concepts are based on the assumption that true professionals have an ongoing self-interest in advancing in the fields to which they've committed their working lives and that they regularly receive and retain evidence that ongoing personal professional achievement is taking place. In this model, the evidence of professional growth and achievement is gathered together by the teacher in the form of a portfolio, not merely for self-gratification, but also for use in competing for whatever rewards in the way of promotion, tenure, or special assignments that such professional documentation might provide. This approach is gaining in popularity as teachers themselves increasingly become the focus of the accountability movement, and they struggle as a profession to prove their professional worth to themselves and to others.

Research has long shown that the recognition of needed change must come from within the teacher, not be imposed from the outside.[7] This model emphasizes teacher-initiated and teacher-regulated inquiry, analysis, and examination, as well as the development of self-supervisory skills for teachers first espoused by Goldhammer.[8] There is a danger in focusing on a supervisor's issues that the teacher's own issues and priorities will be superseded, resulting in a lack of commitment to change on the part of the teacher.[9] The danger is that teachers will adopt a myopic concern for students working for a grade, routinely behaving, and passing proficiency exams—a focus that will subjugate their own concern for true professional fulfillment that is evidenced when student performance exceeds those conventional expectations.

Artists and architects have portfolios of their best work. Doctors and lawyers have client files, papers they've written, and resumes of positions they've held and work that they're particularly proud to have completed. It is this move toward personalized internal supervision that teachers are at long last attempting to emulate. Portfolios give teachers a tangible summation of what they are, what they do, and why they do it.[10] This model is a conscious effort to give teachers opportunities to collect proof of all their accomplishments for personal review and self-assessment. Teachers essentially become their own supervisors and critics through the process of documenting, on an annual basis, what they've accomplished in the forums relevant to their professional performance.

These relevant forums are *classroom, school/district,* and *profession.* What happens in the classroom will always be the most significant parameter of success for teachers because what happens in the classroom is paramount to every teacher's professional success. With this in mind, teacher portfolios should always include evidence of successful teaching. Shulman[11] defines the teaching portfolio as a structured documentary history of a set of coached or mentored acts of teaching substantiated by samples of student work and fully realized only through reflective writing, deliberation, and serious conversation. However, because teachers are also members of a learning community—a school and a school district—other indicators of professional achievement will be evidence that the teacher has made a significant contribution beyond the classroom to one or both of these forums. Finally, teachers are members of a profession, and active participation in that profession through creative, organizational, or leadership contributions should also be part of the self-supervision portfolio. In essence, the portfolio becomes the measure of a well-rounded professional—a collection of artifacts documenting growth through contribution in each of these areas.

What goes into a portfolio will be decided by individual teachers. However, one common approach for introducing and summarizing portfolio contents begins with an updated resume. The process of annually updating one's resume is the cornerstone of professional awareness and self-assessment. If there is nothing new to be added, no new certifications, degrees, curricula, publications, positions, projects, or posts, the year has been one of professional stagnation. True professionals assess and plan for their own career growth on an ongoing basis by taking notice of where they are and setting goals and objectives for where they want to be; the documentation in the portfolio merely provides the evidential details for what is summarized on the resume.

THE METHOD

Exhibit 9-1 gives examples of the types of activities that might be used to underscore growth and achievement in each of the three forums and the type of documentation present in the portfolio. Teachers using this method of professional accountability should have one central file into which all such documentation is placed during the school year and a logbook for ultimately organizing the materials gathered into an easily reviewed collection of professional artifacts. Universities routinely use this approach in assessing professors. Vitae supported by professional dossiers are usually the basis for awarding promotion and tenure in the university setting. The process of collection and review are the focus of both organizational and self-assessment.

Exhibit 9-1 Professional Accountability Portfolio

Forum	Activity	Documentation
Classroom	Exceptional Teaching Lesson Plans Student Achievement Learning Activities	Administrative Evaluations High Proficiency Scores Teaching Awards Student Awards Videotape of Class
School/District	Project Leadership District Service Special Assignments	Project Product Meeting Agendas Letters of Appreciation
Profession	Creative Accomplishments Professional Leadership	Published Books and Articles Agendas Reflecting Organizational Leadership Reports Reflecting Program Direction

Data Collection

This model involves two types of data collection. The first type of data is the type that qualifies a teacher to participate in a portfolio self-supervision program. This model is not for every teacher. Teachers with remediable problems in or out of the classroom should not qualify for self-assessment. These teachers need external guidance in recognizing and addressing identified problems. The Portfolio Self-Supervision Model is designed for teachers with no remediation needs, teachers who simply want to take account of already successful practice and who choose to grow professionally. Therefore, the first type of data required for implementation of this model is qualifying data—proof of exemplary teaching and thorough compliance with all administrative and relational aspects of the teaching position. Excellent evaluations and the absence of complaints from parents, students, or colleagues are essential elements for qualifying to self-supervise.

Once qualified for portfolio self-supervision, the documentation cited in Exhibit 9–1 is a sample of the types of data that can be used to create a portfolio showing growth and achievement. These data can be produced by the teacher, by others, or by the teacher working with others, but it must be objective, observable, and measurable evidence of professional achievement in and out of the classroom. A more complete list of the types of data that would document achievement in each forum addressed by this model follows in Exhibit 9–2. Evidence of successful classroom teaching alone will not be enough to satisfy the requirements of this model. However, documentation of achievement in school/district or profession without documentation of success in the classroom would also not fulfill the requirements of this model. The model, successfully implemented, defines the well-rounded professional, successful both in and out of the classroom.

Conferencing

The teacher is the supervisor in this model. Ideally, there is no need for an external supervisor to "make judgments" regarding the worth or validity of the portfolio or its artifacts. Ideally, issues of external administration should play no role in portfolio supervision.

Exhibit 9–2 Data Documenting Achievement

Classroom	School/District	Profession
Performance Evaluations	Summary of Curriculum Developed	Books
Test Scores	Meeting Agendas	Articles
Parent Letters	List of Programs Developed	Speaking Engagements
Student Awards	List of Programs Led	Association Leadership
Student Test Scores	Letters of Thanks	Awards
Student Programs	Letters of Reference	Degrees
Peer Observations	Board Minutes	Certifications
Taped Observations	Meeting Minutes	Commendations
Teaching Awards	News Releases	Program Development
Summary of New Methods Developed	Newsletters	Professional Travel
Citations	Handouts	Conferences
Student Evaluations	Awards	Appointments to New Posts
Parent Evaluations	Stipends	History of Service on Boards
Summary of New Courses Developed	List of Titles/Appointments	State/National Recognition

Determination of marginal, adequate, or superior performance in the forums of classroom, school/district, or profession in a given year will rest with the teacher or the teacher's choice of outside assessor. Portfolio supervision is a kind of "to thine own self be true" approach. However, there can be a role for an external supervisor in the process. Studies, in fact, show that even highly regarded teachers express a need for external assessment of their accomplishments.[12] To this end, one version of this supervisory process could include an external review of the portfolio itself, conducted by an administrator, a peer, or a personnel specialist. In each case, the reviewer would be asked to render an opinion regarding the quality of the portfolio entries. To avoid the connotation of traditional assessment, however, the review should be in the form of an advisory conference at which the following areas would be addressed:

- Number of Entries
- Quality of Specific Entries
- Areas of Strength
- Areas of Weakness
- Areas To Be Addressed in Future Portfolios

If an administrator conducts the conference, it is essential that all comments be "off the record" and that no written organizational evaluation be part of the process. This supervision model can function as it is supposed to only if it is not connected to any official top-down evaluation plan. Teachers and supervisors must never lose sight that the model's central purpose is to encourage professional *self-supervision*. The model will be successful if teachers, like other professionals, learn to internalize the process of supervising their own professional growth. Reviewers who revert to external assessment will keep this from ever happening. That is why informal discussion of the quality of a portfolio must replace written summative evaluations of its worth. Summative comparison and evaluation of portfolios will take place only when promotion or rewards are at issue.

Even if a peer reviews the portfolio, the process should remain on an informal, informative level. The peer reviewer should act as a professional colleague and mentor commenting on the content and quality of a professional work. What impresses, what concerns, and what begs for development should be the questions addressed, as opposed to what is good and what is bad about the portfolio. In 1995, a task force of the National School Reform Faculty under the aegis of the Annenberg Institute for School Reform created critical friend groups to review teacher portfolios.[13] The critical friend group is a work group, and the portfolios are exhibits accompanied by verbal presentations representing a slice of the work presented.[14] It is hoped that the "unofficial" nature of this presentation and discussion will lead to a frankness and objectivity that "official" assessments and related consequences would discourage. Too often, good teaching vanishes without a trace because teachers have no tradition of sharing, but peer portfolio reviewers are in a unique position to adapt and adopt successful practices documented in portfolios.[15]

If the portfolio is reviewed by a personnel specialist, this collegial aspect of conferencing will be eliminated in favor of an objective, comparative, and competitive analysis. A personnel specialist is one who would review the resume and portfolio with respect to its professional marketability. That is, a personnel specialist is one who reviews resumes and portfolios in terms of applicability and marketability to job searches and promotions. From time to time, it is not a bad practice for teachers, even those who are confident self-supervisors content in current positions, to submit portfolios to personnel specialists for review by applying for positions or promotions for which they qualify. Getting an interview is, in itself, a positive commentary on materials submitted. On the other hand, failure to get an interview can sometimes, although not always, equate with a negative evaluation of credentials. The actual portfolio review conference in this scenario takes the form of a follow-up interview or phone call seeking first-hand feedback concerning the quality of the resume and portfolio submitted. As noted earlier, for self-supervision to be effective, it must align the teacher's perception of performance with reality.

There is also a third type of conferencing that should take place for teachers using this model—self-conferencing or professional reflection. Portfolios can and should contain a section of personal elaboration on a teacher's evolving educational philosophy and professional goals in and out of the classroom. Actually, reflective commentaries on each part of a portfolio are an important part of the process.[16] A teacher portfolio should be more than a miscellaneous collection of artifacts or an extended list of professional activities.[17] The portfolio is the teacher's professional diary—a tangible summary of what they have become, what they have done, and why they have acted as they have during a given school year. It is also the watermark for future professional growth.

TEACHERS MOST LIKELY TO BENEFIT FROM THIS MODEL

Teachers who are new to the profession or who have recognized problems in or out of the classroom will *not* benefit from this model. They have immediate and pressing concerns that require more structured forms of supervision. On the other hand, teachers who are self-confident, professionally mature, and successful will benefit from this model, which requires a high degree of self-discipline and professional responsibility. For most novice or midcareer teachers, the process would be a waste of time and energy needed to become mature, self-disciplined, and confident professionals.

For teachers who do fall into this self-actualizing, achieving category, this may, indeed, be the best possible supervision model because it is designed to accord them their status as true independent professionals. This model does not waste time with the rubric of classroom supervision where none is needed, nor does it invent excuses for supervision in or out of the classroom. This model acknowledges that some teachers are already high-functioning, independent professionals and gives them an intelligent option for determining and monitoring their own professional performance.

PROS AND CONS OF PORTFOLIO SELF-SUPERVISION

One positive aspect of this model not discussed in earlier sections is its potential for encouraging high-level performance. The required annual update of the resume, backed by supportive data, can actually spur professional achievement. There is a certain telling power inherent in self-assessment, particularly for self-starters. These are teachers who got where they are by trying harder, doing more, and striving to perfect what they do. The annual review for such teachers is not an end, but rather a beginning—a starting point for next year's achievement plan. To this end, classroom, school, community, and profession will benefit from the labors entailed in this model. This is a model with the potential for wide impact.

The only real drawback to this model is that even fine teachers have problems from time to time. These problems may be in or outside of the classroom. If this model becomes the *exclusive* approach for supervising some teachers, it can preclude giving them help where and when it is needed. Thus, it becomes important that the self-supervision process remain one of many options and one for which a teacher must qualify on an annual basis. No teacher should ever be thought to be beyond the ken of other supervisory models, and choice of a supervision model must be based on an annual review of data supporting that choice. Professional accountability is not static. It, like the individual professional lives of teachers, adapts to immediate needs and changes with time.

One other criticism of this model is that it will limit administrative control over teacher performance. In an age of increased accountability, administrators and the boards of education that they represent must be sure that the use of this model does not preclude their ability to hold teachers with recognized problems, in and out of the classroom, accountable for their unacceptable performance. This model must be viewed as the exception—not the rule—in supervision. Used inappropriately, it becomes a *carte blanche* invitation for teachers to ignore administratively recognized problems and to overlook subpar performance.

To qualify for self-supervision, teachers must repeatedly show evidence that they have been successful in the ordinary scheme of their daily assignments, in and out of the classroom. Just as the use of earlier models is initiated with data collection showing need for improvement in a given area, so must use of this model be supported by data indicating no such immediate needs. This proof entails exemplary classroom observations and unblemished records in all other aspects of the job description. Again, teachers who qualify for this self-supervision model will be the exception—not the rule—in most schools.

PORTFOLIO SELF-SUPERVISION: A LEGAL PERSPECTIVE

Legally, administrators should be wary of adopting this model in any general or widespread sense. Used indiscreetly, self-supervision can make "official" accountability obsolete and prove to be a virtual "Catch-22," precluding remediation. If the model is used with teachers who do have problems, not only will those problems go unaddressed unless the teacher chooses to address them, but, in addition, teachers facing disciplinary action may maintain that they had no official notice of problems and received no assistance in resolving the problems that gave rise to discipline or dismissal.

Self-supervision without eligibility requirements makes administrative remediation difficult, if not impossible. Self-supervision, under these conditions, is tantamount to allowing an immature teenager with a demonstrated lack of self-control the option of determining a curfew. Thus, to be legally effective, self-supervision must be earned, not optioned.

THEORY INTO PRACTICE ACTIVITIES

1. Update your own resume.
2. Develop a portfolio of data to support your resume entries.
3. Exchange portfolios with a classmate and participate in a conference discussing your resumes and portfolios.
4. Submit your portfolio to an administrator and conference with the administrator concerning the content and quality of your portfolio.
5. Compare the conference you had with a peer in Activity 3 and the conference you had with an administrator in Activity 4. How did they differ? Which was more helpful and why?
6. Apply for a position that would represent a promotion for you. Submit your resume as part of the application process.
7. If you were not called for an interview as a result of your efforts in Activity 6, call the personnel specialist in charge of the application process and ask why you did not receive an interview. Discuss perceived deficiencies.
8. Having updated your resume in Activity 1, plan for the year ahead, setting objectives for achievement in the areas you found yourself needing to improve.
9. Having participated in this model's process, discuss your own perceptions of the model's applicability and value.
10. What did you find most difficult about implementing this model?

NOTES

1. L.W. Barber, "Self-Assessment," in *The New Handbook of Teacher Evaluation*, eds. J. Millman and L. Darling-Hammond (Newbury Park, CA: Sage Publications, 1990), 216.
2. Barber, "Self-Assessment," 220.
3. J.G. Carroll, "Faculty Self-Assessment," in *Handbook of Teacher Evaluation*, ed. J. Millman (Beverly Hills, CA: Sage Publications, 1981), 180–200.
4. C.E. Murray et al., "Rochester's Reforms: The Right Prescription?" *Phi Delta Kappan 79*, no. 2 (1997): 151.
5. Murray et al., "Rochester's Reforms: The Right Prescription?" 151.
6. L. Darling-Hammond, "The Quiet Revolution: Rethinking Teacher Development," *Educational Leadership 53* (6): 4–11.

7. N.J. Boyan and W.D. Copeland, *Instructional Supervision Training Program.* (Columbus, OH: Charles E. Merrill, 1978).

8. R. Goldhammer, *Clinical Supervision* (New York: Holt, Rinehart and Winston, 1969).

9. S.J. Tracy and R. MacNaughton, *Assisting and Assessing Educational Personnel* (Boston, MA: Allyn & Bacon, 1993), 108.

10. K. Cushman, "Educators Making Portfolios: First Results from the National School Reform Faculty," *Phi Delta Kappan 80,* no. 10 (1999): 749.

11. L. Shulman, "Teacher Portfolios," in *With Portfolio in Hand: Validating the New Teacher Professionalism,* ed. N. Lyons (New York: Teachers College Press, 1998), 37.

12. G. Natriello and B. Rowe, *Life in a Loosely-Coupled World,* unpublished paper (St. Louis, MO: Washington University, 1981).

13. Cushman, "Educators Making Portfolios: First Results from the National School Reform Faculty," 745–746.

14. Cushman, "Educators Making Portfolios: First Results from the National School Reform Faculty," 746–747.

15. K. Wolf, "Developing an Effective Teaching Portfolio," *Educational Leadership 53,* no. 6 (1996): 37.

16. Wolf, "Developing an Effective Teaching Portfolio," 36.

17. Wolf, "Developing an Effective Teaching Portfolio," 34.

10

Combining Models

- Differentiating Supervision
- Monitoring the Effectiveness of the Supervision Process
- Conferencing
- Combining Supervision Models: A Legal Perspective
- Theory into Practice Activities

Combining Models

Chris has problems, both in and out of the classroom. Chris has problems maintaining control while trying to present lessons. In addition, Chris seems unable to follow administrative directives. Grades are submitted late, classes are left unsupervised for brief but vital periods of time, and lesson plans are rarely submitted on time.

T his text has introduced an array of distinctly different methods for supervising professional performance. They vary as to philosophy, focus, and procedures, yet each is designed to help teachers fulfill the requirements of their positions more effectively by addressing a range of different problems and needs. Exhibit 10–1 summarizes the models, their focuses, and examples of the problems that they are designed to address.

The introductory scenarios each give examples of teachers likely to benefit from a particular model's approach to supervision; however, there may well be times when a teacher's performance gives rise to concern for more than one kind of issue. When this is the case, the models can be combined in *diversified* individualized supervision plans. For example, the Trait Model may very easily be used with a Performance Objectives Model to address a trait needing identification and improvement. Likewise, a teacher's self-supervision portfolio may include parent and student surveys, reaffirming the teacher's own perception of doing a good job in the classroom, and a summary of a personal performance objective attained by the teacher. Danielson[1] recommends a variety of items for possible inclusion in a portfolio, including unit and lesson plans, knowledge of students and resources, videotapes of teaching, examples of student work, written reflections on lessons taught, and logs on professional service, growth, and research.[1]

Exhibit 10-1 Supervision Model Summary

Model	Focus	Problem Example
Trait	Teacher Traits	Teacher Dress Issue
Process	Structure of Lesson	Poor Lesson Plan
Instructional Objective	Student Learning	Poor Student Work
Teacher Performance Objective	Teacher Performance Out of Classroom	Teacher Tardiness
Self-Supervision	Teacher Concerns	Student Participation
Peer Supervision	In/Out of Classroom	Collegiality Problem
Parent Supervision	Parent Perceptions	Parent Complaints
Student Supervision	Student Perceptions	Student Complaints

The Process Model can also be effectively combined with parent and student surveys to give novice teachers feedback on how they teach and how they are perceived to teach. Are goals and objectives clearly set and presented? Are students given enough time to grasp the concepts presented, and do they feel comfortable asking questions? Is enough time spent in independent practice, and does teacher modeling prepare students for successful independent practice? In response to this feedback, even teachers new to the profession can learn where they need to adjust the process of teaching, and they will be able to set performance objectives for themselves to address areas of need indicated by the surveys.

The Process Model can also be used to supervise veteran teachers whose performance and attention to planning in the classroom need revitalizing. Once again, the teacher and supervisor can use the Performance Objectives Model to direct such a self-improvement plan. The Instructional Objectives Model can also be used with veteran or novice teachers whose classroom performance is missing the mark, i.e., whose students simply are not learning. The Instructional Objectives Model will provide a format for setting objectives and analyzing why some objectives are met and others are not.

Portfolios and self-assessment, although for the most part reserved for teachers without problems, can be implemented at any stage of a teaching career if not used exclusively, in order to develop reflective analysis of professional performance, both in and out of the classroom. That professional performance self-assessment can take place using a combination of other models tailored to individual need. These model combinations can encompass the negotiated methods prescribed by contract while providing additional personalized options that go beyond the contract but do not conflict with it. The goal is to assist teachers to become better at what they do by recognizing where they are in their careers, their skill development, their relational development, and their own personal and professional goal development.

DIFFERENTIATING SUPERVISION

Supervisors encounter a wide range of problems and personalities within the school community. Each problem brings its own unique fact pattern to the fore and illustrates the need for differentiated supervision practices. The profiles that follow in Exhibit 10–2 give 10 examples of the types of fact patterns that a supervisor may have to address. Read the teacher profiles that follow and develop a supervi-

---

Exhibit 10–2 Sample Teacher Profiles

> ### *Profile 1*
> Max has been teaching for five years, and you have observed Max teaching at least five times. During each observation, Max spends an inordinate amount of time lecturing, then has the students begin to do the homework assignment. You find this approach uninspired and notice that many of the students seem bored.
>
> ### *Profile 2*
> Lynn has a reputation as an exemplary teacher. Lynn has taught in the district's high school for 15 years and has won several awards for teaching. However, Lynn is not involved in the school community beyond the classroom. That is, Lynn does virtually nothing beyond

continues

Exhibit 10–2 Continued

the contractual job description to enhance student life. This concerns you because, in a high school environment, there is a need for teachers to do more than simply teach. You have always hired teachers with the understanding that they will play active roles outside the classroom.

Profile 3

Tyler has taught for 25 years, has served on virtually every committee ever convened, and has never missed a day of school. This year, however, you notice a difference in Tyler's performance. Tyler seems to have run out of steam, and students complain that Tyler is short with them and seems disorganized. Fellow teachers hint that they smell liquor on Tyler's breath.

Profile 4

Taylor is a first-year teacher with good self-esteem and great potential. Taylor genuinely enjoys teaching but does not appear to do it well. Parents complain that Taylor's fourth graders have difficulty understanding what is taught. When you have observed Taylor, you notice that each class begins with an activity, but there is no explanation as to what the activity is going to help the students achieve. Taylor justifies this approach as learning through discovery. Nevertheless, the district's achievement tests show Taylor's students achieving far below goals set.

Profile 5

Jo has taught for seven years and is a good teacher, although you wish Jo would incorporate a wider range of learning styles in the lessons you've observed. Several parents have complained that Jo ignores the needs of students who do not culturally identify with Jo. Test scores appear to validate parent concerns.

Profile 6

Gerri is one of three teachers in your building whose students failed all parts of the sixth-grade proficiency test. As principal, you have been ordered to work with Gerri to bring student scores up or to prepare the paperwork for Gerri's dismissal. This is the third year that Gerri's students have performed poorly.

Profile 7

Shawn has taught math for three years in your middle school. When you observed Shawn's class on percentages, you became aware

continues

Exhibit 10–2 Continued

of the fact that Shawn did not know the correct way to convert percentages greater than 100 to whole numbers and fractions.

Profile 8

Brent is new to your school but has been absent at least two days each month. It is now April, and you have noticed that Brent's absences are consistently on the last Friday and Monday of each month. Although your teacher's contract does not give you the right to ask Brent for an explanation or a doctor's note, you feel that you cannot let this trend continue without some comment. How can you incorporate your concern into a supervision plan?

Profile 9

Tiffany has taught at your high school for four years. She was granted tenure last year, and since then, her performance has declined in several respects. For one thing, you are concerned about the way she dresses. Although she is young and relatively attractive, most days she comes to work in tight jeans and jerseys, wearing Gothic makeup. Several parents also report that she is frequently seen socializing with students after school. You are concerned that Tiffany may be courting disaster.

Profile 10

Riley has been an exemplary Latin teacher for the last 20 years. Riley is now 48 and, due to declining enrollment in the program and threatened budget cuts, may not be renewed in the next few years. Riley has been a vital part of your school and an active teacher whom others respect and look to for advice and assistance. As Riley's supervisor, you do not want to lose him, but you see the numbers and the handwriting on the wall that predict the elimination of the Latin program.

Note:

- Data collected determine which supervision model should be used.
- The effectiveness of using a supervision model must be evaluated.
- Data collected following supervision will determine the model's effectiveness.

sion plan for each teacher, using one or a combination of the models presented. Discuss your reasons for choosing a specific plan with a colleague, and determine how you will collect data to support your choice of supervision models. For example, in Profile 1, how will you show Max that too much time is spent lecturing and that students are bored?

MONITORING THE EFFECTIVENESS OF THE SUPERVISION PROCESS

The effect of using a given supervision model to assist a teacher should always be evaluated. A teacher's progress will be determined and measured using the formats and procedures discussed for each model. In each case, specific data will be collected to measure progress. This postprocess data collection should parallel the original data collection justifying the choice of a supervision model. In other words, measurement of progress will be based on looking at the same data that prompted the selection of a supervision model. For example, if concern about a teacher's knowledge of subject matter is borne out by a script of a spelling lesson in which the teacher repeatedly misspells words, measurement of progress using either the Trait or Performance Objectives Model would entail the later collection of lesson scripts in which no further errors are apparent. If parent complaints about teacher communication generate the use of the Client Supervision Model, the absence of parent complaints or a survey showing parent satisfaction would serve as a measurement of this model's effectiveness.

Supervisors should routinely check the effectiveness of their own roles and choices of supervision models by returning to the same data source that guided their choice of supervision model in the first place. This return to the data source applies to both remedial and professional growth supervision. Teachers being supervised using the Self-Supervision or Portfolio Model are those with exemplary classroom and overall professional performance, mature educators with records justifying their ability to monitor their own professional progress. This model choice was justified by good past evaluations of classroom performance, a solid record of continuing professional involvement, parental and student satisfaction, and administrative commendation. To measure progress using this model, teachers should look to updated artifacts attesting to continued exemplary performance in each of these areas, perhaps with additional professional achievements.

The focus of improvement should not change during the period of time in which a particular method of supervision is in place. True progress or lack of progress cannot be measured if that focus changes. Supervisors cannot compare apples and oranges. One central focus based on data will give the process of supervision cohesion and validity.

CONFERENCING

When combining supervision models, it is important to meet with the teacher in a preconference to develop a written plan of supervision linking data collection to each model in the supervision plan. It is also wise to realize that using too many different models can lead to confusion unless the role and purpose of each are clearly understood by both the teacher and the administrator and are spelled out in the plan combining models. That being said, a supervision plan is much like a professional improvement contract. Terms, timelines, resources, objectives, and other relevant conditions should be clearly recorded using the formats accompanying each model. Postconferencing to discuss progress will be based on the terms of the initial plan, all of its accompanying conditions, and data collected to measure progress made.

COMBINING SUPERVISION MODELS: A LEGAL PERSPECTIVE

Each model, as noted earlier, has legal parameters and issues that may have an impact on its effectiveness. Those legal issues and parameters do not go away when models are combined. In fact, the decision to combine models, if not done carefully, may create its own legal issue. Teachers asked to do too much or to address more than one concern at a time may claim confusion as to which issue they should address first and how.

THEORY INTO PRACTICE ACTIVITIES

1. Develop a supervision plan for yourself using at least three of the models discussed.
2. Work with a colleague to implement this supervision plan.

3. Observe a teacher in your building and develop a plan using two of the models that you feel would assist this teacher.
4. Work with at least two other teachers in your building to develop and exchange supervision plans for each other.
5. Implement the plans you develop in Activity 4, and discuss the positives and negatives of actual implementation (i.e., time and logistics).
6. This chapter presented ten teacher profiles as the focus for an exercise in combining models for supervision. In groups of three, compare the plans you have developed, and the supporting data you will use to support your plan and to monitor its effectiveness.
7. Analyze your own district's supervision format and identify one or more models encompassed by that format.

NOTES

1. C. Danielson, *Enhancing Professional Practice: A Framework for Teaching* (Alexandria, VA: Association for Supervision and Curriculum Development, 1996).

CHAPTER

11

Supervising Certified Nonteaching Staff

- Supervising the Guidance Counselor

- The Issue of Confidentiality

- Supervising the School Psychologist

- Supervising the School Nurse

- Supervising the Media Specialist

- Supervising Subject Area Specialists

- Theory into Practice Activities

Supervising Certified Nonteaching Staff

You have just finished a meeting with the very angry parents of a freshman in your high school. They came to the meeting incensed and accompanied by their attorney because they found out that their daughter's guidance counselor had directed her to a family planning clinic where she could receive information on contraception. The counselor's advice came without parent permission or notification. The parents found out about the counselor's actions when the girl's mother discovered birth control pills in her dresser drawer and confronted her. The counselor maintains that the girl asked for the information and that giving it to her seemed to be the right thing to do. The counselor also argues that the student has a right to personal privacy in this matter.

In every school, there is a number of professionally certified staff members who do not teach. They play important supportive roles in the school program but do not have responsibility for the daily supervision of a classroom. Guidance counselors, school psychologists, school nurses, media specialists, and subject area specialists are examples of certified staff in nonteaching positions. These individuals usually hold advanced degrees or training in their areas of expertise and are licensed by the state to practice in that specialty. Although most states view all certified school employees as teachers covered by the collective bargaining agreement, the rights and responsibilities of these certified nonteaching professionals are very different from those of teachers. The job descriptions, trait models, and performance objectives used for supervising the teaching staff do not describe or adequately address the needs of this unique group.

To effectively supervise members of the certified nonteaching staff, supervisors should have a clear idea of the stated mission of each position and should be familiar with the position's job description aimed at implementing that mission. All of these positions provide the opportunity for more independent action and decision making than that found in classroom teaching, unless district policy limits or proscribes that independence. In addition, because of the confidential nature of several of these positions, it may sometimes appear difficult to supervise employee performance. However, lack of clearly stated district policy or supervision in these areas can have dire legal and public relations consequences for districts and administrators.

SUPERVISING THE GUIDANCE COUNSELOR

The roles of the guidance counselor, school psychologist, and school nurse are critical to any school program and fraught with the prospect of controversy. There is an obvious need for confidentiality between these professionals and the students who come to them for advice and help. Students must feel that they can talk freely to these professionals or their roles will become useless. Students must find them readily available and trustworthy or they will not avail themselves of the services that these professionals can provide.

It is this notion of confidentiality and student privacy rights, however, that can often become a focus of the supervisory process. Thus, it is important that a supervisor know the legal rights and responsibilities of guidance counselors and professionals serving in similar roles and that supervisors frame job descriptions, district policies, and trait models that reflect an understanding of these roles in light of the district's own missions for these positions.

THE ISSUE OF CONFIDENTIALITY

Typically, state laws do not address questions related to counselors keeping of information from parents and leave to local school board discretion in the creation of policy in such matters.[1] Except as provided in the Family Educational Rights and Privacy Act (FERPA),[2] a counselor may withhold information from parents.[3] The legislative history of FERPA makes it clear that records made by counselors that remain in the sole possession of the maker and are not accessed or revealed to any other individual except a substitute are not subject to parent disclosure. Educational records do not include counselor or psychologist files that are entirely private and unavailable to other individuals.[4] With this in mind, the counselor in the opening scenario was under no legal obligation to share the student's conversation concerning contraception with her parents.

There are circumstances when public interest concerns will override the privilege of confidentiality. In *Tarasoff v. The Regents of the University of California*, the court found that a psychotherapist had a legal duty, not only to his patient, but also to his patient's would-be victim—both subject to scrutiny by judge and jury.[5] The patient in this pivotal case told his therapist that he wanted to kill Tatiana Tarasoff, but the therapist did not warn her. When the patient carried through with his plan, Tatiana's parents sued the therapist and the university that employed him for negligence. When a student confides an intention to harm another, to commit suicide, or to commit a crime, in light of *Tarasoff*, the counselor's concern for confidentiality is outweighed by society's own interest in preventing a crime or tragedy.

There are, however, other circumstances that may raise parental ire but remain within the penumbra of counselor confidentiality. In the opening scenario, the counselor not only failed to inform the student's parents about her interest in contraception, but he actually referred the student to a family planning clinic. In the eyes of many parents, the counselor in this scenario would appear to be ignoring the rights and responsibilities of the parent in this case. Unfortunately, however, Congress and the courts have weighed in on the side of the student and the counselor in this matter. A 1978 Amendment to Title X of the Public Health and Service Act required that Title X projects offer family planning methods and services to adolescents.[6] Subsequently, the Secretary of Health and Human Services developed regulations requiring that providers of family planning services notify parents or guardians within 10 working days of prescribing contraceptives to unemancipated minors. However, the courts overturned the Secretary's regulatory effort to include parents. The courts found that Congress did not mandate family participation in minors' decision making, instead recognizing that confidentiality is a crucial factor in encouraging teenage use of family planning clinics to stem the epidemic of teenage pregnancies.[7]

A similar line of judicial reasoning has protected counselors who give students information or advice regarding abortion. The question of the need for parental consent was addressed in *City of Akron v. Akron Center for Reproductive Health, Inc.*, where the Supreme Court found a city ordinance prohibiting a physician from performing an abortion on an unmarried minor without the consent of one parent or guardian or without a court order to be unconstitutional.[8] The Court went on to say that state laws or ordinances, when applied to minors seeking abortions without parental consent, must provide alternative procedures whereby the pregnant minor can demonstrate that she is sufficiently mature to make the abortion decision herself or that, despite her immaturity, an abortion would be in her best interest.[9] The controversy in this area continues, but student privacy rights would appear to protect counselors giving advice about abortion and contraception.

If a counselor gives competent advice or refers the student to an appropriate agency, the counselor will not be liable for damages, should the student be injured, but if the school district has a clear policy prohibiting such counseling and the counselor violates that policy, the counselor can be disciplined or, depending on the circumstances, dismissed.[10] School districts have the right to choose curriculum and to develop policy and procedures for every part of that curriculum.

On the opposite side of the ledger, counselors, as teachers, have an absolute obligation to report suspected child abuse. In the National Child Abuse Prevention and Treatment Act, Congress defined *child abuse and neglect* as:

> Physical or mental injury, sexual abuse or exploitation, negligent treatment, or maltreatment of a child under the age of eighteen or the age specified by the child protection law of the state in question, by a person who is responsible for the child's welfare, under circumstances which indicate the child's health or welfare is harmed or threatened thereby.[11]

In developing a plan to supervise guidance counselors, it is important to know what they legally can and cannot do and to understand the district's own rights and responsibilities in supervising the guidance program. Districts can develop policies and job descriptions that proscribe counselors from giving students advice in such controversial areas as contraception and abortion. In the face of a controversy such as the one presented in the opening scenario, a counselor who ignores district policy will be subject to discipline for insubordination. However, if a district has no policy in place to which a counselor can turn in a difficult situation, the district will have no right to second-guess the counselor's own choices.

A legal perspective serves as a backdrop, not an afterthought, for the development of a supervision plan for the guidance counselor. Supervision of these peripheral support positions is frequently lax because building administrators are unsure of how to monitor a student service built on the notion of confidentiality. Obviously, a supervisor cannot sit in on a counseling session, but there are ways in which supervisors can gather objective data to determine whether the performance of a counselor is meeting district expectations. Exhibit 11-1, a Trait Model for supervising the guidance counselor, lists some expectations for the position, with corresponding evidence of performance.

Exhibit 11-1 A Trait Model for Supervising the Guidance Counselor

Responsibility	Evidence of Performance
Individual Student Counseling	Record of Appointments
Crisis Counseling	Anecdotal Reports and Observations
Response to Teacher Referrals	Teacher Complaints and Commendations Teacher Satisfaction Surveys
Group Counseling Sessions	Agendas and Anecdotal Reports
Parent Conferencing	Record of Phone Calls and Conferences
Consultations	Record of Meetings Regarding Students
Supervision of Student Records	Record Review and Complaints
Compliance with Board Policies	Record of Problems and Complaints
Career Planning Activities	Meetings, Agendas, and Anecdotal Reports

SUPERVISING THE SCHOOL PSYCHOLOGIST

The role of the school psychologist, in many respects, parallels that of the school guidance counselor. The psychologist's relationship with students will be subject to the same rules of confidentiality, and the court decisions regarding guidance counselors will also apply to school psychologists. Both are considered counselors. Therefore, psychologists who become aware that a student may harm him- or herself or others do have an obligation to prevent that harm. In addition, school psychologists must be aware of school district policies affecting their practice and must abide by those policies or risk disciplinary action for insubordination.

School psychologists, however, are not school guidance counselors. As practitioners, they are required to have a higher degree of preparation, and they enjoy a higher status in the educational community as a result. However, with this in mind, certified psychologists will be held to higher standards of care and skill than will typical school counselors, and psychiatrists—not usually school employees—will be held to higher standards than will psychologists.[12] The school psychologist will be expected to respond to all situations presented as reasonably as would a similarly trained professional. When problems arise, courts and arbitrators will look at the ways members of the profession have responded to similar situations in order to determine whether the psychologist has acted appropriately.

School psychologists play a central role in a school's special education program. The special education law requires that students be both identified and evaluated.[13] It is the school psychologist who will ordinarily contact and interview parents, and it is the psychologist who will also interview and test students referred for special education services. The psychologist is a central member of the team that will develop an individual education plan for students who qualify for special education.

School psychologists can also play a vital role on a school's Crisis Intervention Team—the group designated to deal with those unforeseen emergencies that have come to plague schools in recent years. Their role on these teams is to deal with aberrant behavior, as well as student reaction to its presence and impact.

In addition, psychologists may play a role in providing consultation and therapy to parents and students in need. The school psychologist is essentially the building's expert resource in dealing with the emotional and social impact that the problems of the twenty-first century have on public schools.

With this understanding of the role of the school psychologist, the Trait Model shown in Exhibit 11–2 has been developed to serve as a guide for supervising the performance of the school psychologist.

SUPERVISING THE SCHOOL NURSE

The school nurse shares the concern for confidentiality discussed regarding the guidance counselor and the school psychologist. All deal with the kinds of intimate personal problems that pose liability risks for the district and the personnel in charge. Unless a student has reached the age of maturity recognized by a given state, however,

Exhibit 11–2 A Trait Model for Supervising the School Psychologist

Area of Responsibility	Evidence of Performance
Student Evaluation	Documented Reports
Participation in the Special Education Process	Record of IEP Team Activity
Participation in Crisis Intervention Process	Observation and Anecdotal Record
Compliance with District Policies and Procedures	Complaints and Documented Records
Parent Consultations	Calendar and Conference Record
Student Therapy	Calendar and Conference Record
Teacher Consultations	Conference Record and Teacher Response
Compliance with State and Federal Law	Timely Submission of Reports
Record Keeping	Clear, Timely, Annotated Records
Professional Growth	Course Work and Workshops

the nurse has an obligation to contact the parents regarding any health problems that a student presents. Supervision of required immunization and health screening are an integral part of what the school nurse does, in addition to dealing with the routine health problems that students present on a daily basis.

School nurses, like other certified school employees, should be licensed to practice; trained in the skills needed to screen and diagnose; and ready, willing, and able to administer aid on a short-term basis to students and teachers in medical travail. Legally, they are responsible for the physical well-being of students while they are at school, but they do not have the right to prescribe treatment without parental notification and permission. With parent permission, the school nurse can administer drugs and medication that a student may require during the school day, but the school nurse may not prescribe medication without documented parent permission to do so.

Some school systems use the school nurse to provide targeted programs in health and well-being. School nurses who teach will bring health issues to the classroom and discuss procedures for maintaining physical stamina.

It is important that teachers and school staff be made aware of student health problems that may interfere with a student's ability to participate fully in the school program. It is particularly vital that staff be informed regarding the potential for life-threatening emergencies that may occur during the course of the school day. On a regular basis, the school nurse must inform and update teachers on the physical condition of the students they will be teaching.

The Trait Model shown in Exhibit 11–3 addresses some of the areas involved in supervising the school nurse.

SUPERVISING THE MEDIA SPECIALIST

The job of the media specialist is quite different from those of the guidance counselor, school psychologist, and school nurse. Confidentiality is not an issue for the media specialist, but student First Amendment rights are. Media specialists are responsible for school libraries and all that they entail in this era of computerized and mechanized learning. A legal perspective on the role of the media specialist, however, would reveal the role to be ministerial and reactive where boards of education exercise their right to be proactive

Exhibit 11-3 A Trait Model for Supervising the School Nurse

Area of Responsibility	Evidence of Performance
Health Screenings	Student Records
Immunization Checks	Student Records and Problems
Parent Contacts	Recorded Calls and Conferences
Ministering to Student Needs	Record of Visits and Treatment
Drug Administration	Drugs Administration Record
Health Instruction	Record of Presentations
Office Cleanliness	Observations
Ability To React to Emergencies	Observations
Staff Notification	Record of Notices and Problems
Compliance with Laws and Board Regulations	Recorded Problems and Complaints

and discretionary. In essence, the Supreme Court has given school boards broad discretion to create school districts that reflect the legitimate and substantial community in promoting respect for authority and traditional values, be they social, moral, or political.[14]

The job of the media specialist involves the selection, control, and distribution of supplementary learning materials. However, if a board chooses to become involved in the selection of instructional materials for the media center, the courts will uphold its right to do so. Twice the courts have upheld a school board's right to remove books from its media center, noting that a book does not acquire tenure and, therefore, can be removed by the same authority that made the initial selection.[15] Only if boards' censorship has been found to be motivated by a desire to suppress controversial positions have courts struck down their attempt to control the content of the media center.[16] The courts have recognized an inherent tension between the school board's two essential functions of exposing young minds to the clash of ideologies in the free marketplace of ideas and instilling basic community values in our youth.[17] Internet use is the next frontier for the media specialist. In 1996, Congress enacted the Communications Decency Act, making schools, libraries, and other institutions criminally liable if they allow children electronic access to obscene material, but this and similar state legislation has come under constitutional scrutiny.

Essentially, the media specialist's job can be very controversial if boards of education fail to exercise their right to create policy regarding the selection and distribution of media material within a district. Media specialists get into trouble when they are forced to second-guess school boards in selecting materials for center distribution.

The Trait Model for supervising the Media Specialist shown in Exhibit 11–4 assumes that the board of education will exercise its right to select and control media distribution.

Exhibit 11–4 A Trait Model for Supervising the Media Specialist

Area of Responsibility	Evidence of Performance
Selection and Ordering of Materials	List Submitted for District Approval
Maintenance of Media Center Budget	Budget Submission
Maintenance of the Media Center	Observation and Report of Problems
Development of Media Center Programs	Reports and Agendas
Compliance with Board Rules and Regulations	Evidence of Problems
Encouragement of Media Usage	Programs and Use Records
Equipment and Resource Inventory	Prescribed Reports
Faculty Updates and Inservices	Program Records
Classroom Presentations on Media Usage	Lesson Plans
Personal Professional Development	Record of Training

SUPERVISING SUBJECT AREA SPECIALISTS

The reading specialist, the math specialist, and the Title I teacher all belong in this category of certified nonteaching staff, in that they do not have regular classroom assignments. Their role is that of assisting teachers. The subject area specialist is presumed to have expertise in a particular area of the curriculum. It is this specialist's role to provide teachers with information regarding changes in the teaching of given subjects.

For example, language arts teachers would be expected to be familiar with both the phonics and whole-language approaches to the teaching of reading. More importantly, they would be expected to help the teachers to apply one or both approaches effectively in their classrooms. Title I teachers would be expected to have an expertise in addressing the needs of students who are either emotionally or academically deprived. The role of the subject area specialist becomes controversial only if the promised expertise is not there or if methodology is espoused without board approval. A Trait Model for supervising subject area specialists is shown in Exhibit 11–5.

The Trait Model should in no way be the exclusive means for supervising personnel in these certified but nonteaching roles. When problems or deficiencies are recognized, performance objectives are an appropriate plan for addressing supervisory needs. In addition, parent, teacher, and student surveys can provide valuable information regarding outside perception of this phase of the school program. Finally, peer supervision by the teachers who are to be served by these support programs can provide telling data regarding their effectiveness.

THEORY INTO PRACTICE ACTIVITIES

1. What other positions can you identify that would fit into this category?
2. Develop Trait Models to supervise staff in these positions.
3. How are guidance counselors supervised in your school?
4. Who supervises the subject area specialists in your school?
5. Who supervises your school nurse?
6. Review your district's job descriptions for the positions discussed in this chapter.

Exhibit 11–5 A Trait Model for Supervising the Subject Area Specialist

Area of Responsibility	Evidence of Performance
Program Supervision	Student Achievement
Program Coordination	Classroom Observations
Assistance to Classroom Teachers	Teacher Complaints and Commendations
Faculty Training	Record of Inservice Presentations
Consultations	Record of Conferencing with Teachers
Program Evaluation	Student Performance; Teacher Satisfaction
Compliance with Board Policies	Problems and Controversies
Personal Professional Development	Course Work and Research
Research and Planning	Documented Reports
Program Budgeting	Documented Budgets

7. Discuss any problems that your district has encountered in supervising staff in these areas.
8. Evaluate the effectiveness of your school's guidance program.
9. Are the subject area specialists in your district effective? Why or why not?
10. How can supervision of certified nonteaching staff in your district be improved?

NOTES

1. L. Fischer and G.P. Sorenson, *School Law for Counselors, Psychologists, and Social Workers* (New York: Longman, 1985), 20.
2. 20 U.S.C. § 1232g (1996); 34 C.F.R. Section 99 *et seq.* (1996).
3. Fischer and Sorenson, *School Law for Counselors, Psychologists, and Social Workers*, 20.
4. 120 Cong. Rec. 27, 36533 (1974).
5. 551 P.2d 334 (Cal. 1976).

6. 42 U.S.C. § 300(a).
7. Planned Parenthood Federation of America, Inc. v. Heckler, 52 U.S.L.W. 2028 (July 8, 1983).
8. 51 U.S.L.W. 4767 (1983).
9. City of Akron v. Akron Center for Reproductive Health, Inc., 51 U.S.L.W. 4767 (1983).
10. Fischer and Sorenson, *School Law for Counselors, Psychologists, and Social Workers,* 58–59.
11. 42 U.S.C.A. Section 5101 (1996).
12. Fischer and Sorenson, *School Law for Counselors, Psychologists, and Social Workers,* 70.
13. P.L. 94–142 § 300.530 (b).
14. Board of Education, Island Trees Union Free School District No. 26 v. Pico, 457 U.S. 853 (1982).
15. *See* Bicknell v. Vergennes Union High School Board of Directors, 638 F.2d 438 (2d Cir. 1980); Presidents Council, District 25 v. Community School Board No. 25, 457 F.2d 289 (2d Cir. 1972), *cert. denied,* 409 U.S. 998 (1972).
16. *See, e.g.,* Case v. Unified School District No. 233, 908 F.Supp. 864 (D. Kan. 1995); Wexner v. Anderson Union High School District Board of Trustees, 258 Cal. Rptr. 26 (Ct. App. 1989), *review denied,* No. S010543 (Cal. 1989).
17. Seyfried v. Walton, 668 F.2d 214 (3rd Cir. 1981).

12

Supervising Extracurricular Staff and Programs

- Athletic Staff and Programs
- The Method
- Performance Groups and Programs
- Publication Advisors and Programs
- General Activity Advisors and Programs
- Conclusion
- Theory into Practice Activities

Supervising Extracurricular Staff and Programs

The Drama Club's director has decided that this year the group will present "Equus." The football coach refuses to let girls try out for the team. The advisor to the school newspaper has authorized an article on teen pregnancy and abortion, based on interviews with past and present students with first-hand experience. A male teacher at the high school has offered to serve as the advisor to a new gay men's group.

E xtracurricular programs are part of the life of every school. They can also become an ongoing administrative headache if left unsupervised. Administrators, preoccupied with supervising a district's academic programs, often adopt a policy of benign neglect with respect to the extracurricular programs that they come to regret. Unfortunately, a study of school case law will show that a sizeable number of major legal cases arises in the context of extracurricular programs. With this in mind, this chapter will discuss the legal perspective on what advisors and coaches can and cannot do in extracurricular programs and will use that perspective as a focus for their corresponding supervision plans.

There are four basic types of extracurricular programs:

1. Athletic Groups and Programs
2. Performance Groups and Programs
3. Publication Groups and Programs
4. General Activity Groups and Programs

To supervise each program effectively, administrators should have a clear understanding of the types of problems that can arise in implementing each program, as well as an understanding of the day-to-day administrative demands of each extracurricular program. Once again, job descriptions will become the basis for supervision. The job description is, after all, the official notice of job requirements, prescriptions and proscriptions, and expectations that an arbitrator or court will use to decide any controversies that may develop during the course of employment. Thus, it is important that administrators and those charged with supervising extracurricular staff do informed planning when developing extracurricular job descriptions.

In some instances, the negotiated agreement may also play a role in determining how extracurricular positions will be supervised. Tenure in a given position need never become a factor unless it is negotiated into the contract, and one-year appointments are one way that districts can maintain control over unsatisfactory performance in these positions. However, if tenure or the methods of supervision/evaluation are part of the negotiated agreement, these provisions will direct the course of supervision, discipline, and evaluation. As noted earlier, arbitrators and courts will both look first to the contract for guidance in controversies.

As school districts set about the task of developing job descriptions for extracurricular positions and negotiating contracts that cover these positions, case law addressing problems in each of the four extracurricular areas noted can help districts to create job descriptions, contracts, and policies that will guide the supervision of extracurricular staff and programs. Forewarned is forearmed, and school case law identifies the areas of extracurricular responsibility and performance that have drawn judicial notice.

ATHLETIC STAFF AND PROGRAMS

There are many requirements and responsibilities that can be included in a coach's job description, and there are always questions about what coaches can and cannot do. However, it is helpful to know which rights, requirements, responsibilities, and questions the courts have already been asked to review and how they have ruled when faced with suits charging negligence or infringement of student rights. Such judicial foresight should guide the development of coaching job descriptions and will keep school districts and coaches in charge and out of court. The following coaching responsibilities and rights are addressed by the judicial rulings cited.

1. A coach should know the sport and provide proper instruction.
Coaches should have knowledge and experience in the sport assigned and be able to provide proper instruction. Just as knowledge of subject matter is a part of every teacher's job description, so

should knowledge of a given sport, preferably through experience, be an essential element of every coach's job description. Unfortunately, there is no certification requirement for coaches that would ensure school districts that they had received proper training in the sport they are to coach. Districts are forced to rely on records and reports of personal participation. In many cases, with a growing dearth of trained adults willing to coach, school districts feel that they can't be too particular. However, coaches who do not understand a sport, its methodology, and its physical demands open a district up to tort liability, should a student be injured while participating.

Students who participate in a district's athletic program are owed a duty of care that includes proper instruction and supervision by a knowledgeable coach. If students are entrusted to a coach who does not properly instruct and supervise, that duty of care is breached. Additionally, if, as a result of poor instruction and supervision, a student is injured, a district can be liable for negligent tort. In hiring coaches who are not properly trained and experienced in a given sport, a district breaches its legal duty to protect participating students from unreasonable risks of harm. Injury is a foreseeable danger if students are not properly instructed about how to use equipment and perform safely. A coach's commission of an improper act or a coach's failure to act both expose the coach and district to charges of negligence. For example, in one case, a court upheld a charge of negligence, finding that a duty existed on the part of the coach to provide a catcher's mask and to instruct in its proper use.[1]

2. A coach should comply with state and regional athletic association rules and regulations.

State and regional athletic associations have developed rules addressing recruitment, eligibility, age, and other issues regulating student and district participation in competitive league play. The courts have found these rules and regulations to be a legitimate effort to equalize competitive conditions and to protect the health and safety of younger, less experienced students engaged in a sport.[2] For example, the Supreme Court of Oklahoma upheld a league rule that barred students who reached their nineteenth birthday by September 1 from participating in interscholastic sports because it found that older and more mature athletes could be a threat to the health and safety of younger students participating in the same competitive activity.[3] With this in mind, coaches have a duty to comply with association and league rules.

3. A coach should comply with the district's policy linking athletic participation to academic performance.
Schools have a primary duty to educate, and, to that end, many schools have conditioned extracurricular participation in sports on satisfactory academic performance. "No pass, no play" provisions are common at both state and local levels, and the courts have upheld the right of districts to premise extracurricular participation on classroom performance. Such rules have been found rationally related to a legitimate interest in providing quality education to all students.[4]

4. A coach should set standards for conduct on and off the field.
A primary goal of every athletic program must be to inculcate behavior standards endorsed by the school and community. Supporting this goal, courts have routinely upheld student suspensions for smoking and drinking.[5] On a more serious note, the Third Circuit upheld a student's 60-day suspension for smoking marijuana and drinking beer on school property.[6] The court in this case and others found that students had no property interest in participating in extracurricular activities, and that the suspension was a reasonable way to discourage student drug use.[7] Therefore, school districts and the coaches who represent them have the right and responsibility to set reasonable behavioral expectations for students and to condition student participation in team sports on compliance with those expectations.

5. A coach should maintain and use equipment safely.
If students do not have the proper equipment to participate safely in a sport or if that equipment is not properly maintained, there is a foreseeable risk of injury and a breach in the district's duty of care to student athletes. In one case, for example, a coach who modified a school's whirlpool but failed to install a ground fault interrupter was found liable for the electrocution death of a student who used the whirlpool.[8]

6. A coach should set and maintain a reasonable training schedule.
Coaches often condition participation in formal competition upon student attendance at practice sessions, games, and performances. In general, the courts have upheld a coach's right to set such rules for participation.[9] The courts have seen such coaching directives as rationally related to the discipline goals of sport programs.

7. A coach may prescribe special grooming regulations as conditions for participation if based on legitimate health and safety issues.[10]
An Alabama court upheld a coach's "clean shaven" policy because it did not deprive students of any constitutionally protected right and was aimed primarily at presenting the school in a favorable light.[11]
8. Coaches should not discriminate on the basis of gender when selecting students to participate in team sports.
Title IX gives school districts the right to sponsor separate teams for members of each sex where selection is based on competitive skill or where the activity is a contact sport.[12] However, Title IX also says that:

> Where a recipient [school district] operates or sponsors a team in a particular sport for members of one sex but operates or sponsors no such team for members of the other sex, and athletic opportunities for members of that sex have previously been limited, members of the excluded sex must be allowed to try out for the team offered unless the sport involved is a contact sport.[13]

Courts have rejected the attempts of coaches and school districts to keep women from participating in contact sports. Title IX, as can be seen above, permits but does not require that women be refused the opportunity to participate in contact sports. As a result, many women have challenged coaches and school districts that have denied them this right. Courts have rejected the argument that denial was justified on the basis of protecting the health and safety of the women, essentially finding that women wishing to participate should be given the opportunity to show that they are as fit or more fit than the weakest male member of the team.[14]
9. Coaches should serve as role models for students.
Coaches work with students in highly charged and competitive forums. In this environment, coaches have a professional responsibility to act with restraint and wisdom in all circumstances. Coaches who lose sight of their responsibility to act as role models for the students in their charge have been duly punished by the courts. A high school wrestling coach who involved students in a false "weigh-in" prior to a wrestling meet was found guilty of "immorality," and his termination was upheld.[15] In a similar vein, a male high school

coach was also terminated for immorality for taking female athletes to a bar, sleeping in a hotel room with them, and engaging in sexual involvement with female students over a 20-year period.[16]

10. Coaches should be sure that all students have passed prescribed physicals before allowing participation in sports programs and should monitor chronic physical problems that may affect student health and safety during participation.

A clean bill of health from a student's family physician should be a prerequisite for participation in any sports program, and it is the duty of the coaching staff to be sure that all students comply with this rule. In addition, students who are injured or who develop health problems while participating should be watched and monitored so that conditions and injuries are not exacerbated by their participation in sports activities. Coaches who fail to monitor and adjust program involvement to accommodate a student's health concerns may be guilty of negligence if the student's injuries or health problems are aggravated by participation in the program. In a Louisiana case, for example, a coach was found negligent because he permitted an athlete to continue playing when the neck roll that the student was required to wear to keep from aggravating an injury was dislodged. The coach knew about the injury, and the student's parents had stipulated that he wear the neck roll.[17]

THE METHOD

To supervise coaches effectively, districts should not only make them aware of district requirements for the position, but also orient them to district expectations and explain the reasons for the requirements used to supervise the coaching staff. Coaches who are aware of the legal liability that attaches to their actions and inactions are more likely to act with prudence and restraint. Orientation sessions should be a required part of the supervision process, not an optional one.

As with all methods of supervision, the method used with coaches should be based on data documenting performance in each area. Exhibit 12–1 lists the type of data that correlates with each area of responsibility discussed.

If coaches exhibit problems in any of these areas, those problems are likely to be remediable and, therefore, subject to supervision, i.e., improvement with assistance. Coaches can be put on notice of

Exhibit 12–1 A Trait Model for Supervising Coaches

Area of Responsibility	Data Documenting Performance
Knowledge and Proper Instruction	Observation, Record of Problems/Injuries
Compliance with Association Rules	Complaints and Cited Problems
Compliance with District Academic Regulations	Reports from Teachers and Observations
Maintenance and Safe Use of Equipment	Accident and Injury Reports
Grooming and Behavior Standards	Team Appearance and Behavior in Competition
Title IX Compliance	No Evidence or Complaints of Discrimination
Maintenance of Standards of Conduct	Discipline Referrals for Athletes
Role Modeling	Complaints from Parents and Teachers
Monitoring Student Health and Safety	Records and Observations

where their performances are unsatisfactory, and they can be given job targets and specific directions for overcoming deficiencies in each of these areas of responsibility.

There are, however, aspects to the job of coaching that elude remediation through such direct supervision. Successful coaching is often a combination of luck and charisma. Thus, school districts must decide whether "success" measured by "winning" will be another requirement of the job, and, if it is, the question then becomes one of how to assist a coach in producing a winning team. There is no easy answer to this question. If there were, all teams would be winners.

PERFORMANCE GROUPS AND PROGRAMS

Under this heading, one would include groups such as the school band, orchestra, dance ensemble, drama club, and art club. These groups exist to train students in skill areas in the performance arts and to provide opportunities for them to perform for the public under the auspices of the school program. Performance groups and programs such as sports are an integral part of most school programs, often extensions of curricular offerings. As such, the courts have accorded schools a wide berth in controlling how these groups are managed and what they perform. The Supreme Court has said that school authorities can censor student expression in school-related activities, as long as the censorship decisions are based on legitimate pedagogical concerns.[18] The Court reasoned that public forms of student expression in sponsored programs appear to bear the school's imprimatur and, therefore, that the school has a right to censor, consistent with its educational objectives.[19]

A major question in supervising the advisors to performance groups and the programs themselves then becomes one of determining a balance between the advisor's academic freedom and the district's right to control sponsored programs. A teacher's academic freedom includes the right to experiment with new ideas and to select methods and materials However, the Supreme Court has ruled that local school boards must be permitted to establish and apply their curriculum in such a way as to transmit community values because there is a legitimate and substantial community interest in promoting respect for authority and traditional values, be they social, moral, or political.[20] Extracurricular performance programs are usually part of existing curricular programs, and curricula are board controlled. In one recent case in point, the Fourth Circuit found that a high school teacher did not have a First Amendment right to select a controversial play to be performed by students in her advanced acting class.[21]

Job descriptions for advisors to performing groups can and should include the requirement that programs sponsored by the school, like the curricula, receive administrative approval before teachers begin planning implementation. Teachers do not have a First Amendment right to determine what instructional materials to use; that control is placed with school boards.[22] Although the concept of academic freedom has been recognized by the courts, it has never conferred on teachers the control of the public school curricula.[23] Performance groups, as an extension of the public school curricula, are subject to school board control. Forewarned advisors who ignore a requirement for prior approval would be guilty of insubordination and subject to disciplinary action.

However, boards of education that do not exercise their right to control the content of the curricula and allied extracurricular programs will lose that right. An Iowa court, for example, found that a high school drama teacher's choice of plays that included scenes with drinking and profanity were constitutionally protected when a school district had no school rules or prior notice requirements that such plays were not allowed.[24] Advisors who receive no adequate notice or direction from the board of education concerning prohibited conduct cannot later be punished for the decisions with which the board disagrees. To do so would have a chilling effect on their ability to function in their roles as advisors.

A Trait Model for supervising advisors to performance programs might include the responsibilities listed in Exhibit 12–2. Exhibit 12–2 also lists some of the corresponding data for monitoring performance.

As with coaches, performance program advisors are also most successful when they have the elusive charisma that instills students with commitment and confidence, but charisma, like a winning season, is not easily subject to supervision.

PUBLICATION ADVISORS AND PROGRAMS

School newspapers, literary magazines, and yearbooks are just a few of the principal publications that showcase students and their expressive written achievements. School publications foster student creativity, research, and responsibility, but they also have the potential for fueling controversy regarding the limits of student free expression. In 1988, in *Hazelwood School District v. Kuhlmeier*, the Supreme Court gave school authorities the right to censor student expression in school publications, as long as the censorship decisions are based on legitimate pedagogical concerns.[25] The principal in this landmark case deleted two pages from the school newspaper that contained articles about divorce and teenage pregnancy because the principal feared that individuals could be identified in the articles. The Court in this case rejected the idea that a school newspaper or any school activity becomes a public forum for student expression unless school authorities clearly *intended* it to be. The Court rea-

Exhibit 12-2 A Trait Model for Performance Program Advisors

Area of Responsibility	Pertinent Data
Selection of Approved Performance Programs	Administrative Approval Submissions
Supervision of Planning and Production Meetings and Rehearsals	Observations and Complaints
Skill Development	Observations and Response to Performance
Development of Public Relations Program	Publications and Communications
Knowledgeability in Performance Area	Program Observations and Evaluations
Ability To Develop Team Work	Observation and Program Evaluation
Ability To Secure Funding	Funding and Budget Reports
Ability To Budget Wisely	Budget Reports
Ability To Organize Successful Programs	Observations and Public Support
Ability To Bring Projects to Fruition	Observations and Evaluations

soned that student expression in a school newspaper *represents* the school and appears to bear the school's imprimatur; therefore, school authorities have broad discretion to ensure that such expression is consistent with the school's educational objectives.[26]

The Court's position regarding a school district's right to control publications under its sponsorship plays a central role in the supervision of publication advisors and programs. At issue is the duty of the advisor to protect the interests of the school, as represented by a given publication, while helping students to create, express themselves, and learn responsibly. This is no easy mission but is an essential part of the job description for publication advisors. Advisors who are unwilling or unable to exercise the control called for by *Hazelwood* will expose the school district to public controversy and litigation.

Mindful monitoring of student expression is not the only potentially controversial responsibility of publication advisors. School publications in need of financial support frequently sell advertising that can also become a source of controversy. In 1989, for example, Planned Parenthood sued a school district because the district denied the group's request to advertise in the school newspapers, yearbooks, and programs for athletic events. Planned Parenthood claimed that the district's decision violated the group's free speech rights. The Ninth Circuit Court of Appeals, however, concluded that the district had the right to reject Planned Parenthood's request because the advertisements were inconsistent with the district's educational mission and might interfere with the proper function of education.[27]

Issues of student and sponsor censorship are best addressed prospectively, rather than retrospectively, by boards of education. Although the courts have given boards of education the right to control the content of school publications with which they will be identified, boards are wise to exercise that right before controversy arises by developing job descriptions and orientation programs that make advisors aware of board rights and advisor responsibilities in the development of school-sponsored publications. Relitigating *Hazelwood* should not be one of the advisor's objectives. Exhibit 12–3 is a Trait Model for supervising publication advisors that explicates a board of education's expectations for this position.

This Trait Model for publications advisors provides a brief outline of some of the central responsibilities entailed by these positions. Those who supervise these positions can use this list to develop appropriate job targets if problems evolve. Job targets should address particular problems that have been observed and provide specific suggestions (i.e., conditions for addressing these problems, as well as ways in which improvement will be measured).

GENERAL ACTIVITY ADVISORS AND PROGRAMS

Most public schools host a variety of clubs and groups not associated with the curricular program. These social and interest groups, too, have come to the attention of the courts in recent years, and school districts that understand these decisions can avoid disruptive controversy and relitigation. These decisions can provide insights in

Exhibit 12–3 A Trait Model for Supervising Publication Advisors

Areas of Responsibility	Data Monitoring Performance
Instruction in Writing and Research	Quality of Publication
Instruction in Publication Ethics	Complaints and Controversies
Preview of All Published Material	Record of Approvals and Denials
Ability To Meet Publication Deadlines	Publication Record
Ability To Manage Publication Budget	Budget Record
Ability To Promote Readership	Record of Projects and Readership Rates
Regular Evaluation of Publication	Record of Needed Reforms
Ability To Promote Student Involvement	Student Membership
Ability To Foster Creativity	Review of Publication
Promotion of the School's Mission	Publication Review and Evaluation

the development of job descriptions that will form the basis for supervising the role of club advisors acting as agents of the school district.

The Supreme Court has held that the right of free association is implicit in the freedoms of speech, assembly, and petition.[28] By joining together with others with similar views, individuals make their own views more effective.[29] Students often initiate clubs and groups with open membership to attract others with similar interests and to foster social exchange or the development of expertise in these areas of interest. Unfortunately, student-initiated clubs with open membership may not always reflect traditional community interests and values. Schools may be reluctant to sponsor a Gay Men's Group, a Young Communist's Society, or a Dungeons and Dragons Club.

The rule of thumb for school districts in this area was provided by the Equal Access Act, which stipulated that if federally assisted schools provide a limited open forum for noncurricular student groups to meet during noninstructional time, access cannot be denied to specific groups based on the religious, political, philosophical, or other content of the groups' meetings.[30] School districts create limited open forums whenever they allow any student group not related to the curricular program to meet during noninstructional time. If, however, districts allow only student groups related to the curriculum to meet during noninstructional time, they can retain control over the use of the school building by unauthorized and unrelated student-initiated clubs. For example, in 1996, the Salt Lake City School Board adopted a district-wide policy that denied access to all noncurricular student groups, following a request by the Gay-Straight Alliance to hold meetings at a high school.[31] Once a limited open forum exists, the only other instance in which school authorities can restrict the formation of student-initiated clubs meeting during noninstructional time is if there is a threat of disruption.[32]

Districts that create limited open forums can assist advisors to student-initiated clubs and curriculum-related clubs by requiring that clubs develop constitutions and mission statements directing and clarifying the focus of their activities. As with athletics, school districts can also have policies conditioning extracurricular participation on maintenance of a designated grade point average.[33] The courts have found that grade point restrictions are rationally related to the school's concern for academic excellence.[34]

The range of student-initiated and curricular-related clubs that fall into this general activity category is limitless. Nevertheless, some clubs will be more prestigious and membership more competitive. The National Honor Society, a curriculum-related club, for example, requires students to provide evidence of achievement in several areas, and nomination for membership is frequently based on faculty review and endorsement. The courts have upheld subjective selection for such clubs, as long as the procedures developed are applied fairly and equitably.[35] Students do not have a property right at stake in connection with selection for such competitive groups.[36]

In supervising advisors to these general activity clubs, orientations and handbook guidance at the onset are vital. Advisors need to know what is expected of them in this role, and they need to understand their duties regarding fundraising, field trips, guest speakers, building use, and the sundry other issues that will affect the club's functioning. Exhibit 12–4 captures a few of the general responsibilities that affect most club advisors. Job descriptions for these positions should develop more specific role expectations.

CONCLUSION

The National Center for Education Statistics has found that four of five seniors participate in some extracurricular activity.[37] Extracurricular activities are a big part of every school program, and the advisors in charge of implementing them require and deserve effective supervision. Schools that are proactive in assisting advisors by developing rules and policies for extracurricular programs will be supported by the courts. However, schools that are reactive, responding to crises created by careless supervision, are destined to defend the choices they make.

Exhibit 12–4 A General Trait Model for Club Advisors

Responsibilities	Performance Data
Develop Club Mission Statement	Written Mission Statement
Develop Club Constitution	Written Constitution
Help Students Develop Meeting Agendas	Record of Agendas
Help Students Set Relevant Objectives	Record of Club's Objectives
Help Students Attain Objectives	Minutes of Meetings
Arrange for Relevant Activities	Journal of Club Activities
Manage Club Resources	Budget Records
Assist with Needed Fundraising	Record of Fundraising Activities
Benefit the School or Community	Narrative Description of Efforts
Enhance Student Skills	Showcase Club Efforts/Products

THEORY INTO PRACTICE ACTIVITIES

1. Develop a list of athletic staff and programs presently in your building.
2. Who supervises these employees, and what forms and procedures are used?
3. Develop a list of all performance groups and their respective advisors.
4. How are these advisors and programs supervised?
5. Develop a list of all publication programs and their respective advisors.
6. How are these advisors and programs supervised in your building?
7. What general activity programs are offered in your building?
8. How are these groups and their advisors supervised?
9. How are the advisors and coaches for all of these various extracurricular programs selected, and how long are their contracts?
10. Discuss any problems you are aware of with the supervision of these groups.

NOTES

1. Parisi v. Harpursville Central School District, 553 N.Y.S.2d 566 (App. Div. 1990).
2. *See, e.g.,* Arkansas Activities Association v. Meyer, 805 S.W.2d 58 (Ark. 1991); Thomas v. Greencastle Community School Corporation, 603 N.E.2d 190 (Ind. Ct. App. 1992).
3. Mahan v. Agee, 652 P.2d 765 (Okla. 1982).
4. Spring Branch Independent School District v. Stamos, 695 S.W.2d 556 (Tex. 1985), *dismissed,* 475 U.S. 1001 (1986).
5. *See, e.g.,* Braesch v. DePasquale, 265 N.W.2d 842 (Neb. 1978), *cert. denied,* 439 U.S. 1068 (1979).
6. Palmer v. Merluzzi, 868 F.2d 90 (3d Cir. 1989).
7. See also Zehner v. Central Berkshire Regional School District, 921 F.Supp. 850 (D. Mass. 1995).
8. Massie v. Persson, 729 S.W.2d 448 (Ky. Ct. App. 1987).
9. *See, e.g.,* Keller v. Gardner Community Consolidated Grade School District, 72C, 552 F.Supp. 512 (N.D. Ill. 1982).
10. *See, e.g.,* Menora v. Illinois High School Association, 683 F.2d 1030 (7th Cir. 1982), *cert. denied,* 459 U.S. 1156 (1983).

11. Davenport v. Randolph County Board of Education, 730 F.2d 1395 (11th Cir. 1984).

12. 34 C.F.R. § 106.41(b)(1996).

13. 34 C.F.R. § 106.41(b)(1996).

14. See, e.g., Lantz v. Ambach, 620 F.Supp. 663 (S.D.N.Y. 1985); Saint v. Nebraska Activities Association, 684 F.Supp. 626 (D.Neb. 1988).

15. Florian v. Highland Local School District Board of Education, 493 N.E.2d 249 (1983).

16. Strohm v. Reynoldsburg City School District Board of Education, Case No. 97APE07–972, 1998 Ohio App. LEXIS 1375 (Franklin Co. AP, Mar. 31, 1998).

17. Harvey v. Ouachita Parish School Board, 674 So.2d 372 (La. Ct. App. 1996).

18. Hazelwood School District v. Kuhlmeier, 484 U.S. 260 (1988).

19. See DeNooyer v. Merinelli, 12 F.3d 211 (6th Cir. 1993), cert. denied, S.Ct. 1540 (1994).

20. Board of Education of Island Trees School District v. Pico, 457 U.S. 853 (1982).

21. Boring v. Buncombe County Board of Education, 136 F.3d 364 (4th Cir. 1998).

22. Fisher v. Fairbanks North Star Borough School Dist., 704 P.2d 213 (Alaska 1985).

23. Kirkland v. Northside Independent School District, 890 F.2d 794 (5th Cir. 1989), cert. denied, 496 U.S. 926 (1990).

24. Webb v. Lake Mills Community School District, 344 F.Supp. 791 (N.D. Iowa 1972).

25. Hazelwood School District v. Kuhlmeier, 484 U.S. 260 (1988).

26. DeNooyer v. Merinelli, 12 F.3d 211 (6th Cir. 1993), cert. denied, 114 S.Ct. 1540 (1994).

27. Planned Parenthood v. Clark County School District, 887 F.2d 935 (9th Cir. 1989), rehearing en banc, 941 F.2d 817 (9th Cir. 1991).

28. Healy v. James, 408 U.S. 169 (1972).

29. State Board for Community Colleges and Occupational Education v. Olson, 687 P.2d 429 (Colo. 1984), appeal after remand, 759 P.2d 829 (Colo. Ct. App. 1988).

30. 20 U.S.C. § 4071 (1996).

31. Karen Diegmueller, "Salt Lake City Prepares List of Banned Clubs," Education Week, May 1, 1996, 3.

32. See, e.g., Dixon v. Beresh, 361 F.Supp. 253 (E.D. Mich. 1973).

33. Thompson v. Fayette County Public Schools, 786 S.W.2d 879 (Ky. Ct. App. 1990).

34. See, e.g., Rousselle v. Plaquemines Parish School Board, 527 So. 2d 376 (La. Ct. App. 1988).

35. Price v. Young, 580 F.Supp. 1 (E.D. Ark. 1983).

36. Karnstein v. Pewaukee School Board, 557 F.Supp. 565 (E.D. Wisc. 1983).

37. National Center for Education Statistics, Extracurricular Participation and Student Engagement, National Education Longitudinal Study (Washington, DC: U.S. Department of Education, 1995).

13

Supervising Preservice and Substitute Teachers

- Preservice Supervision

- Screening Potential Student Teachers

- Screening Cooperating Teachers

- Supervising Student Teachers

- Supervising Student Teachers:
  A Legal Perspective

- Screening Substitute Teachers

- Supervising Substitute Teachers

- Supervising Substitute Teachers:
  A Legal Perspective

- Theory into Practice Activities

Supervising Preservice and Substitute Teachers

As a student teacher, Fran worked with a mediocre field advisor. When Fran graduated and was licensed to teach, there were no prospective openings. Now, a month of working as an itinerant substitute teacher has Fran feeling that, on most days, work as a substitute amounts to babysitting. Fran had hoped that work as a substitute would be more meaningful and instructive for the students assigned but poor or nonexistent lesson plans, inadequate instructions, the lack of seating charts, and the absence of any visible adult mentor have replaced the joy of becoming a teacher with the daily challenge of being a substitute.

I n this day and age of schools under siege because of an increasing awareness of potential violence, there should be no unsupervised adult working in any capacity in a public school. Every adult working in a school should have a clearly defined purpose in being there. For teachers, administrators, and support staff, that purpose is usually spelled out in the job descriptions for each position. Unfortunately, the roles of student teachers and substitute teachers are seldom clearly defined or acknowledged. All too often, building administrators know nothing about the adults serving in these shadow roles. Many building administrators see them as welcome "warm bodies" to take up the slack for missing teachers. However, the danger inherent in this attitude of benign neglect should be obvious and the need for a supervision plan immediate. What parent would leave a child alone in a room with an unsupervised perfect stranger? However, that is exactly what schools, acting *in loco parentis*, do every time they allow an unsupervised student teacher or substitute teacher to take over a public school classroom.

PRESERVICE SUPERVISION

Preservice training, or student teaching, is the culminating field experience in most teacher education programs. Students seeking teaching licenses are required to take course work in the field of education, including at least one course involving them in first-hand classroom apprenticeships. Classroom experience is intended to give prospective teachers the opportunity to put theory into practice under the supervision of a willing practitioner.

Over time, the length of the student teaching period has grown from a few weeks of several hours to half- and full-day experiences for a full term or semester, and the forum for student teaching has moved out of the university's on-site laboratory school into the public school classroom. Universities now collaborate with public school teachers in preparing the next generation of teachers. These changes, however, come with both good news and bad news. The good news is that the presence of student teachers in the classroom causes cooperating teachers to reexamine their methods, procedures, and management approaches.[1] The bad news is that cooperating teachers often assume supervisory responsibilities for which they have little or no formal training.[2]

Both selection of student teachers and selection of the cooperating teachers who will supervise them lack clear procedures and rigorous gatekeeping. Other than the establishment of grade point average (GPA) requirements, most universities have avoided personality, psychological, and character issues in deciding who can student teach, because they fear the legal ramifications associated with denying a student who has taken all the required courses the opportunity to student teach.[3] The responsibility for screening students before allowing them to student teach, however, should not rest solely with the university. School districts have both a right and a responsibility to screen potential student teachers also. Screening should be the first element of district supervision, and the screening process should extend to potential cooperating teachers, as well as to potential student teachers. Just as not every college student who has completed the prescribed courses in a teacher education program should be given free rein in an actual classroom, not every practicing teacher is capable of providing the kind of instruction and supervision expected of a cooperating teacher. Indeed, in the 1980s, many states began to implement special teacher requirements for serving as a co-operating teacher.[4]

SCREENING POTENTIAL STUDENT TEACHERS

In the spirit of collaboration, school districts tend to accept the judgment of universities in placing prospective student teachers. However, school districts should retain and use their right to reject student teachers with questionable credentials. Exhibit 13-1 lists some of the basic credentials that should be open to review by the district and the corresponding types of data that could be used as the basis for accepting or rejecting a student teacher.

Usually, prospective student teachers do not have a work record that can be used to evaluate their potential to perform effectively. Their work record is the transcript, their record of performance in the courses preparing them for the student teaching experience. Although grades may not always predict exemplary performance as a teacher, the fact that a college student has not done well in preparatory course work cannot be dismissed as a predictor of problems. Lack of understanding in relevant subject areas, lack of commitment, or sheer laziness will come to the fore with poor grades. Administrators who allow student teachers with poor grades to take over classrooms should question why they have chosen to do so. The paying customer is the student, not the student teacher or the uni-

---

Exhibit 13-1 Screening Student Teachers: Reviewable Credentials and Data

Reviewable Credentials	Data Documenting Credentials
Criminal Records Check	Fingerprint and Record Check
Preparation for Classroom Teaching	Transcript of Courses Taken
Ability To Understand and Use Theory	Grades Received in Courses Taken
Ability To Relate Well to Students and Teachers	Letters of Reference/Personality Screenings

versity. Every student deserves the best possible teacher available at all times.

A criminal records check is now a must in many states for any person responsible for the care, custody, or control of a child.[5] Student teachers fall into this category and should be required to undergo a background check before their assignment to a school is approved. In most states, employees who have been convicted of or have pled guilty to criminal offenses may not be employed by a board of education.[6] Although student teachers are not hired employees, if they are allowed access to the children in a school and a child is injured as a result of that access, the liability of the school district for the wrongs committed by this person could be staggering.[7]

Because student teachers are strangers to the school, it is not unreasonable to require that they provide letters of reference supporting their ability to conduct themselves appropriately and to relate well to those with whom they've been required to work in the past. Some districts use tested interviewing systems, such as the *Gallup Perceiver Interviewing System*, to identify teacher personality and attitude traits that portend success in the classroom.[8] These researched techniques, presently used in hiring procedures, can easily be adapted for use in screening student teachers. One positive result of using such procedures is that exposure to this screening process provides student teachers with insights into the interviewing and hiring processes that school districts actually use. Another positive offshoot of this approach is that student teachers who do well can become potential job applicants in the district in which they have trained.

SCREENING COOPERATING TEACHERS

Districts also need to become involved in the selection of the teachers who will work with and ultimately supervise the student teachers that a district accepts. Studies have shown that cooperating teachers are the most crucial factor in the development of competent student teachers.[9,10] The job of a cooperating teacher is by no means easy. The cooperating teacher is role model, mentor, teacher, and disciplinarian to the student teacher. The cooperating teacher must deal effectively with both the tangibles and intangibles of teaching another adult. That is, the cooperating teacher must share technique, subject matter, and strategies while also being sensitive to the neophyte's corresponding need to share ideas, feelings, and fears.

There probably should be training and licensing programs for co-operating teachers. However, attempts to develop such programs have failed for lack of incentives.[11] Cooperating teachers are not usually paid for their role in training student teachers, although some universities provide the opportunity for course work free of charge as an incentive. Nor does the district reimburse cooperating teachers for their efforts. Thus, over time, the rewards for acting as a cooperating teacher have become basically intrinsic. Cooperating teachers enjoy the opportunity to share their expertise and to refine what they themselves do in the classroom by watching someone else's approach.

There is, however, a "fly in the ointment" of this collaboration, in that cooperating teachers who are not skilled or ethical can use the opportunity to work with a student teacher as a personal invitation to take a break from the demands of classroom teaching. Unethical cooperating teachers can equate practice teaching with preservice dues-paying or veritable slavery, an attitude that benefits neither the student teacher nor the students. Districts that exercise no control over the process of selecting cooperating teachers risk the prospect of the "blind leading the blind." With this in mind, it becomes essential that building principals supervise the selection of cooperating teachers, as well as student teachers.

Some of the characteristics that should be used in determining whether a practicing teacher is ready to mentor a novice are listed in Exhibit 13–2, with the supporting data that can be used to justify approval or rejection by the building administrator.

Only teachers who are both experienced and successful should be allowed to mentor student teachers. Experience alone should not qualify one to act as a cooperating teacher. At present, many district administrators are not involved in the process whereby cooperating teachers link up with universities seeking mentors for student teachers. As a result, unqualified teachers undertake the instruction and supervision of unscreened student teachers, and the blind lead the blind into pedagogical oblivion, or worse.

Once collaboration between the university and the school has been established, the university supervisor should assume overall supervisory responsibility for student teaching.[12] However, wise building administrators should continue to check with the cooperating teacher concerning the status of the student teacher. The cooperating teacher becomes the student teacher's official supervisor, an agent of

Exhibit 13-2 Screening Cooperating Teachers: Reviewable Credentials and Data

Reviewable Credentials	Data Documenting Performance
Exemplary Teaching Performance	Evaluations and Student Performance
Personal Academic Accomplishments	Degrees, Licenses, and Honors
Years of Successful Experience	Employment Record
Success in Working with Others	Projects, Committees, and Grants

the school district for both legal and instructional purposes, but a visit from the building's administrator during the student teaching period will give the student teaching experience a valuable dose of reality.

SUPERVISING STUDENT TEACHERS

Cooperating teachers should use all of the models presented to supervise student teachers at one time or another during the student teaching period. As prospective job applicants, student teachers should understand all of the various responsibilities of the job of teaching and the various ways in which school districts can monitor their performance. The Trait Model is an outline of pertinent personal and professional characteristics deemed important. The Process Model is an explication of research, describing the best way to plan and execute a lesson. The Instructional Objectives Model reminds student teachers that the ultimate measurement of teacher performance will always be student achievement. The Performance Objectives Model describes the way in which specific areas of concern (i.e., job targets) will be described and how achievement of those targets will be measured. The Peer Supervision Model draws the novice teacher's attention to the importance of peer respect and input in the development of the total professional. Parent and Student Supervision Models highlight customer satisfaction, a factor with vital implications for the future of public education. The Portfolio, or Self-Supervision Model, emphasizes the need for setting personal goals in all relevant areas to gain a sense of true professionalism. Each has a place in the supervisory process, and each can be used instructively with student teachers. In each instance, it will be important to explain the focus of the model, the way that data will be collected to support the use of a particular model, and the way that the student teacher will be supervised using the model. Used effectively, the models give student teachers a progressive perspective of their role as professional teachers.

SUPERVISING STUDENT TEACHERS: A LEGAL PERSPECTIVE

There are legal ramifications to participating in the supervision of student teachers. These legal ramifications affect building administrators and cooperating teachers. If student teachers were job applicants, the district would have a duty to screen applicants to ensure that they did not have criminal records and posed no threat of injury to the students to be entrusted to their care. The district's duty of care does not change simply because student teachers are not actual job applicants. Student teachers will still be spending unsupervised time with students and can pose a risk to students if they have prior records of criminal behavior. Either the district or the university must accept the obligation of screening student teachers to dispel this risk. Districts, building administrators, or university supervisors who fail to screen student teachers expose students to the risk of criminal behavior and themselves to charges of negligence, should students be injured by student teachers.

It is also important to emphasize that student teachers are not certified or licensed to teach as regular teachers. Therefore, it is illegal to use them as substitute teachers. Some states, such as Kansas, specifically prohibit student teachers from serving as regular or substitute teachers while student teaching.[13] Even when state law appears to allow a student teacher to act as a substitute, school districts must remember that they will be legally vulnerable, should something go wrong. If a student is injured on a student teacher's watch, the injured student's lawyer can be expected to argue that "but for" the assignment of an unlicensed teacher, the injury would not have occurred.

Student teachers are in the school to learn by doing, but they are neither licensed nor paid employees and should not be used as substitutes for paid and licensed teachers. On the positive side of the legal ledger, however, neither cooperating teachers nor school districts can be legally liable for their evaluations of student teachers. The law supports honest appraisal. Cooperating teachers who are faced with supervising poorly performing student teachers can minimize controversy by doing the following:

1. Write statements of fact rather than opinion, and write objective, rather than subjective, descriptions of the student teacher's behavior.
2. Limit the information recorded to that which is relevant to or affects the student teacher's performance in the classroom.
3. Avoid public disclosures about the student teacher's deficiencies.
4. Avoid any verbal or nonverbal suggestions of malice or intent of harm.
5. Limit the likelihood of bad faith or ill will charges by communicating concerns for both the student teacher's welfare and the school's welfare.[14]

If a cooperating teacher documents poor student teacher performance objectively and without malice, the cooperating teacher should have no fear about rendering a negative evaluation and keeping a poorly performing student teacher out of the classroom. The cooperating teacher will not be guilty of defamation because the cooperating teacher is exercising "qualified privilege." That is, the teacher is immune if the statement is made in good faith, on a proper occasion, from a proper motive, in a proper manner, and based on reasonable or probable cause.[15] Evaluations communicated to the student teacher and the student teacher's university supervisor for the purpose of noting concerns during a conference with the student teacher and supervisor and based on documented data are not defamatory. Cooperating teachers must refrain, however, from discussing student teachers with anyone outside this circle of confidential communication.

SCREENING SUBSTITUTE TEACHERS

Substitute teachers, in contrast to student teachers, are paid and licensed employees of the school district. As such, they are subject to all of the state and local rules and regulations governing the school and are agents of the local board of education. Substitute teachers take the place of regular teachers who cannot cover their classes, and, just as regular teachers must be certified in the area to which they are assigned, so, too, should substitute teachers be certified in their areas of assignment. The process for screening substitute teachers, like that for preservice teachers, should begin with a criminal background check. However, unlike a student teacher, a substitute will usually have a work history as a substitute that can be checked to determine the substitute's reliability and effectiveness in the classroom, as well. Exhibit 13–3 lists other credentials that should also be used before hiring a substitute.

The itinerant nature of substitute teaching makes it especially important for school districts to screen prospective substitute employees. Substitutes, like regular teachers hired by a district, become agents of the district, making the district directly liable for any injury that students or other employees may incur at their hands. Districts that do not screen prospective substitutes before hiring may be found guilty of negligent hiring for not exercising reasonable care in screening prospective substitutes before placing them in the classroom.[16]

Districts can make substitute teaching less transient by establishing a coterie of permanent substitutes who report for work as regular teachers in a building but without established classroom assign-

---

Exhibit 13–3 Screening Prospective Substitute Teachers: Reviewable Credentials and Data

Reviewable Credentials	Data Sources
Eligibility to Teach	Certificate or License
Employment History	Application for Employment as a Substitute
Background	Fingerprinting and Criminal Records Check
Educational Preparation	Transcripts and Grades
Successful Teaching Experience	References

ments. These teachers would be hired with the understanding that they would stand in primarily for regular teachers in their areas of certification, and, if this were not possible, they would supervise study halls for students of absent teachers in areas for which they were not certified. On days when no teachers were absent, these substitutes could be used to relieve regular teachers in their certification areas as needed for peer supervision activities or to tutor students in need of extra help in their subject areas.

There are several real advantages beyond the obvious to having a coterie of permanent substitutes assigned to a building:

1. These teachers can work with the teachers for whom they are substituting in advance of the need for subbing to develop emergency lesson plans that will be timely and relevant to the curriculum.
2. These teachers will know the school, the teachers, and, most importantly, the students, thereby mitigating or eliminating many of the problems that arise when a teacher is a stranger to a building.
3. Effective substitutes can be a ready source that a district turns to when replacing regular teachers who resign or take leave. Building administrators will have had the opportunity to see first-hand the quality of their work.
4. Schools will be more prepared to address the staffing emergencies that regularly arise.
5. Substitutes will have the opportunity to learn their craft in a stable environment in which they have a future investment—the potential for placement in a regular position.

SUPERVISING SUBSTITUTE TEACHERS

The first step in supervising substitute teachers is to give them notice of district, building, and teacher expectations. Substitute teachers, like other employees, cannot be expected to perform without adequate notice of what is expected. There are three sources of notice for substitute teachers:

1. Prehiring orientation
2. Student and teacher handbooks
3. Emergency lesson plans

Schools should plan ahead for substitute coverage. It is inevitable that subs will be needed during the school year. Therefore, it is expedient to invite prospective substitutes to an orientation that is part of the preliminary hiring process. At this orientation, subs will have a chance to tour the building, meet teachers and administrators, learn about procedures and conditions unique to the building, and receive student and teacher handbooks.

For substitutes hired later in the school year, a videotape of this initial orientation and packets of relevant handbooks and materials can relieve the stress of reporting for duty that first morning. In addition, it helps to appoint regular teacher mentors to check with the substitute throughout the day to be sure that all is going as expected.

Emergency lesson plans that are complete and possible to implement are the most important element of substitute supervision, and this is an element that the administrator in charge can control. It should be a part of every regular teacher's job description to submit up-to-date emergency lesson plans each week—lesson plans that set instructional objectives for the students in keeping with the prescribed curriculum. Lesson plans should also include accurate seating charts and notations addressing any special concerns, such as student health or behavior problems of which the substitute should be aware.

If substitute teachers are hired in the traditional way, i.e., on a day-to-day basis, a combination of the Trait Model and Instructional Objectives Model is the best approach to supervision. The forms used for each method of supervision can be part of the orientation materials that substitute teachers receive, so that they know what will be expected. These same forms and procedures, discussed in earlier chapters, should then become the basis for a debriefing at the end of the substitute's day, a brief conference with either the administrator or a peer mentor, reviewing data documenting outcomes and performance perceptions. This material will then be used by the regular teacher to plan for lessons on the teacher's return.

The Instructional Objectives Model gives structure to the regular teacher's emergency plan and a "road map" for the substitute. It will include a clear statement of the lesson's objective, the conditions under which students will pursue that objective, expected student behavior, and a means of measuring student achievement that the regular teacher can use for planning subsequent lessons.

SUPERVISING SUBSTITUTE TEACHERS: A LEGAL PERSPECTIVE

The use of substitute teachers makes districts legally vulnerable on several fronts. The substitute teacher is a paid district employee, an agent of the school district. As such, the district will be liable for any injuries that the substitute may cause in the course of employment. In particular, districts will be liable for any injuries to students or staff that occur as the result of poor screening.

Once hired, districts are also responsible for providing substitutes with timely notice of job expectations and all peripheral information needed to meet those expectations. Lack of proper notice can be used as an excuse for a great many wrongs. However, it becomes difficult to provide proper notice when employees come and go through the revolving door of substitute hiring. With the move to include special needs students in regular classrooms, proper notice takes on an entirely new dimension of importance.

Districts can find themselves liable for failing to inform substitutes fully about students requiring special medical attention or about potentially disruptive and dangerous students or circumstances. In *Ferraro v. Board of Education of City of New York*,[17] for example, the principal failed to inform a substitute teacher that one of the students that the sub would be supervising had a record of assaulting other students. As a result of the principal's oversight, the student did assault another student while both were in the care of the substitute. A jury found the principal's failure to inform and warn the substitute constituted an act of negligence that was the proximate cause of the assault and resulting injury. They ruled that liability on the part of the defendant board of education, based on the principal's negligence, was amply shown.

There are two ways to avoid potential problems with substitute teachers. One is to develop the coterie of permanent substitute teachers, a stable and integral part of the work force, as described earlier. The other is to assign responsibility for all aspects of the supervision of substitute teachers to one administrator, with the understanding that this person would screen, orient, inform, update, supervise, and evaluate substitute teacher performance. This administrator would be responsible for essentially supervising a staff within a staff and for troubleshooting any potential problems.

THEORY INTO PRACTICE ACTIVITIES

1. How are preservice teachers placed in your district, and how many are presently working in your district's schools?
2. Interview local universities in charge of preservice programs and find out what requirements student teachers must meet before they are placed in a school.
3. How often does the university supervisor visit the student teacher in the field?
4. Describe the procedures the university supervisor uses to monitor student teacher performance in the field.
5. How are teachers chosen to supervise student teachers during their field experience?
6. What role does the school's principal play in the placement and supervision of student teachers in your school?
7. Interview a supervising teacher, and discuss the procedures the supervising teacher uses in order to assist assigned student teachers.
8. Interview two student teachers concerning their perception of the university's supervision.
9. Interview two student teachers concerning their perception of the field teacher's supervision.
10. Were the student teachers you interviewed required to undergo a criminal background check before placement, and were they interviewed by school district personnel before placement?

NOTES

1. E. Guyton, "Working with Student Teachers: Incentives, Problems, and Advantages," *The Professional Educator 10*, no. 1 (1987): 21–28.
2. M.A. Moorehead et al., "A Model for Improving Student Supervision," *Action in Teacher Education 10*, no. 1 (1988): 39–42.
3. W.S. Hopkins and K.D. Moore, *Clinical Supervision: A Practical Guide to Student Teacher Supervision* (Madison, WI: Brown & Benchmark Publishers, 1993), 9.
4. M. Haberman and P. Harris, "State Requirements for Cooperating Teachers," *Journal of Teacher Education 33*, no. 3 (1982): 45–47.
5. *See, e.g., Ohio Revised Code* § 3319.39(A)(1).
6. *See, e.g., Ohio Revised Code* § 3319.39(A)(3).

7. R.W. Rebore, *Personnel Administration in Education: A Management Approach* (Needham Heights, MA: Allyn & Bacon, 1995), 113.

8. The Gallup Organization, *Teacher Perceiver: Interview Process,* (Lincoln, NE: The Gallup Organization, 1996).

9. I.L. Pfeiffer and J.B. Dunlap, *Supervision of Teachers: A Guide to Improving Instruction,* (Phoenix, AZ: The Oryx Press, 1982).

10. E. Guyton, "Guidelines for Developing Educational Programs for Cooperating Teachers," *Action in Teacher Education 11,* no. 3 (1989): 54-58.

11. Hopkins and Moore, *Clinical Supervision: A Practical Guide to Student Teacher Supervision,* 11.

12. Guyton, "Guidelines for Developing Educational Programs for Cooperating Teachers," 54-58.

13. M.A. Henry et al., *Supervising Student Teachers the Professional Way,* 3rd ed. (Terre Haute, IN: Sycamore Press, 1982).

14. V. Helm, "Defamation, Due Process, and Evaluating Clinical Experiences," *Action in Teacher Education 4,* no.2 (1982): 27-32.

15. Baskett v. Crossfield, 228 S.W. 673 (Ky. 1920).

16. Massey et al., Labay et al., Devericks et al. v. Akron City Board of Education, 82 F.Supp.2d 735; 2000 U.S. Dist. LEXIS 896 (January 19, 2000).

17. 212 N.Y.S. 2d 615, *affirmed,* 221 N.Y.S. 2d 279 (App. Div. 1961).

CHAPTER

14

Supervising Administrators

223

Supervising Administrators

Taylor is the principal of a large urban middle school with many problems. Students at the middle school are not academically attaining state standards, teachers have complained that discipline is inconsistent, and parents fear for the safety of their children in what they perceive to be a chaotic environment. Taylor has been the middle school principal for five years, and things are getting worse.

N o supervision plan is complete if administrators, frequently cast in the role of supervisors, are not themselves supervised. Supervisors benefit from careful analysis of their own supervisory patterns and interactions.[1] Good administrators do far more than turn the school's lights on in the morning and turn them off again at day's end. Good administrators, in general, are essential to making and keeping schools effective. For instance, effective schools are said to have principals who are viewed as instructional leaders, providing guidance, support, and encouragement to staff when requested.[2] Although no two administrators function or get results in the same ways, there are fundamental management approaches that are subject to analysis.[3]

This chapter will explore three different approaches to supervising administrators. Although there exists a variety of administrative positions with wide-ranging areas of responsibility, this discussion will focus on principals. The supervision methods discussed, however, can be adapted to any administrative position using the administrative position job description to personalize the process.

Principals are the single most influential factor in promoting excellence in education.[4] Principals are charged with "seeing the big picture" and coordinating the efforts of teachers, students, parents, and support staff to achieve district goals and objectives. Each performance area, influenced by the goals of the system and building unit, has its own special job targets for the principal.[5] Redfern[6] identified at least seven performance areas on which principals should be evaluated:

1. Instruction
2. Organization and Administration
3. Personnel Management
4. Pupil Personnel Management
5. Business Management
6. Community Public Relations
7. Program Development

Methods used to supervise the work of principals should prioritize the tasks most critical to a principal's success in each of these areas, just as supervisors prioritize the elements of classroom teaching that must be addressed, based on observation.

In preparing to supervise administrators, districts must answer three questions:

1. Who should supervise administrators?
2. What should be supervised?
3. How should supervision be conducted?

WHO SHOULD SUPERVISE ADMINISTRATORS

Ultimately, the task of supervising all district administrators, including principals, rests with the superintendent, the district's CEO; however, the superintendent can delegate the task of supervisory data collection and assistance to a variety of other agents. Traditionally, the superintendent evaluates all building principals based on data received from assistant superintendents, teachers, parents, students, support staff, and community. Each of these sources plays a role in one or more of the seven target areas for principal supervision and develops a perception of principal performance through first-hand experience. Thus, in a very real sense, each supervises the principal's performance. In a similar fashion, the building principal will evaluate assistant principals and other building-level administrators, based on data and information from these same sources, as well as from the building principal's first-hand experience and perceptions formed directly in the workplace.

WHAT SHOULD BE SUPERVISED

The job of principal is multifaceted, and there is a variety of opinions regarding the focus of supervision. The seven areas noted above are relatively vague and general parameters for supervision. Exhibit 14-1, however, gives examples of specific data sources that could be used to document performance in each area.

Exhibit 14-1 Principal Performance Areas and Data Sources

Performance Area	Data Relevant to Supervision
Instruction	Test Scores, Grades, Awards, Retention Rates Parent, Student, Teacher Satisfaction Surveys
Organization Administration	Documented Problems, Report Promptness, Building Appearance, Evidence of Teamwork
Personnel Management	Grievance Record, Staff Attendance Records, Workers Compensation Claims, Complaints
Pupil Personnel Management	Student Activity Program, Counseling Program, Special Education Program, Complaints from Parents, Students, and Teachers.
Business Management	Budget Records, Assignment of Staff, Provision and Conservation of Resources, Innovative Programs, Grant Funding
Community Public Relations	Community Programs, Newsletters, News Releases, Record of Building Use, Presence on Community Boards and Committees
Program Development	Staff Development, Orientations, Curriculum Revision and Implementation, Evidence of New Approaches in Any of the Other Areas

In addition to these job function areas, it can be argued that principals should be evaluated with respect to those often-elusive public relations skills and qualities that play a vital role in defining leadership success. After all, principals are hired for more than their ability to organize, manage, develop, and maintain. Interpersonal skills and the ability to respond intelligently to whatever issues arise always play a significant role during the administrative interview and in the decision to hire. In actual fact, principals will be unable to organize, manage, develop, and maintain building functions without creating a persona evoking most of the personal characteristics listed in Exhibit 14–2. The problem is that these characteristics are subjective factors not easily defined or measured. Nevertheless, Exhibit 14–2 attempts to capture some of the possible data sources that might be used to measure a principal's effectiveness in these elusive relational areas. These data sources can be documented through anecdotal descriptions of a principal's observed performance in given situations (sometimes resulting in commendations or reprimands); surveys measuring parent, student, and teacher perceptions of the principal's performance; and records addressing specific administrative activities, such as grant writing, budgeting, or program development, that a principal is called upon to produce.

The ways that a principal responds to the board, the press, the public, difficult parents, and teachers will be obvious over time. Few administrations are problem free, and the memory of particularly poor and particularly effective performances becomes part of the anecdotal history of a given principal's administration.

Principals, unlike teachers, are almost always discretionary employees. That is, they are not protected by a collective bargaining agreement. Principals retain their positions at the discretion of the board of education and can be removed from their positions with far less effort than that needed to remove tenured teachers. Still, the job of a principal is far too complex and unpredictable to be described in legally binding detail. Recent changes and additional responsibilities also are often accompanied by considerable ambiguity.[7] This ambiguity requires principals to make decisions and to act in a discretionary, rather than ministerial, capacity. They must often make decisions using their own best judgment, as opposed to following an existing rule or direction from a superior. Such independent thinking and action is always a risky business and gives a dou-

Exhibit 14–2 Principal Personal Characteristics and Data Sources

Personal Characteristics	Data Documenting Performance
Intelligence	Problem Solving
Leadership	Successful Projects
Creativity	New Programs, Grants, Problem Solutions
Enthusiasm	Reputation among Teachers, Students, Public
Honesty	Grievance Record, Reputation
Poise	Performance in Difficult Situations
Stability	Reputation, Situational Response Record
Health and Stamina	Attendance Record
Flexibility	Situational Response Record
Personal Appearance	Anecdotal Record

ble-edged meaning to the concept of discretionary employment. Exhibit 14–2 provides an outline of the kinds of behaviors that can be used to document the elusive characteristics that ultimately describe a principal's discretionary behavior and to determine whether that behavior complies with the board's own expectations.

HOW SHOULD PRINCIPALS BE SUPERVISED

Once a decision has been made concerning the areas that will be supervised and the types of data that will be used to direct supervision, there are at least three methods for assembling pertinent information and using it to assist principals to improve their performances.

A Trait Model for Administrators

In education, it is assumed that once a man or woman is appointed to an administrative or supervisory post, he or she will be able to function satisfactorily without further direction, but there is a gap between assumption and reality here.[8] Principals, like teachers, should be given notice regarding the specific requirements of their positions. Although the seven areas of supervision cited above and their corresponding data sources provide an outline for supervising principals, specific job expectations should be the starting point for supervision, and a list of administrative traits and objectives, patterned on the Trait Model for teachers in Chapter 3, can keep the supervision process from becoming arbitrary and capricious. Administrators, like teachers, should have the opportunity to review the instrument that will be used to supervise them, and this instrument should detail the job expectations.

The degree to which job expectations were met should also be an element of administrative supervision. Unlike teachers, administrators do compete for positions and promotions on a regular basis. Therefore, their degree of success in a particular area, as compared with administrators in similar situations, is relevant to the supervision process. With this in mind, a numerical scale awarding points for performance can take the ambiguity out of the process.

Because the degree of success plays such a vital role in the career advancement of principals, it becomes important to explain point awards with documentation justifying point assignments. Orientation materials for new administrators, now sorely lacking, should be developed to explicate examples of superior, mediocre, and marginal performance with accompanying documentation. Such orientation materials can go a long way toward filling that knowledge gap that most new administrators encounter in knowing what is expected of them. Exhibit 14–3 provides an example of the kinds of traits that can be used to define expectations in each of the seven areas noted.

Examples of principals performing in superior, mediocre, and marginal ways in each area can also assist principals and eliminate the subjectivity that inevitably accompanies an effort to describe performance with a trait. For instance, a principal performing marginally in the area of *providing for technologic growth* can be objectively described as not yet having unpacked the computers sent to the building last July. A principal performing in a satisfactory but mediocre way would have unpacked the computers, assembled a computer lab, and sent one interested teacher to a workshop to learn what to do with the lab. In contrast, superior performance

Exhibit 14–3 A Trait Model for Principals

Area of Supervision	Trait or Data Illustrating Performance
Instruction	Students perform well on state exams. Executes innovative and effective curriculum. Evidence of individual student success.
Organization Administration	Promptly submits all requested reports. Complies with all district directives. Keeps good records.
Personnel Management	Communicates well with staff. Settles problems at the building level. Promotes low staff absenteeism.
Business Management	Develops appropriate and timely budgets. Maintains a clean building. Seeks grants to supplement budget.
Community Public Relations	Communicates well and often with public. Responds to parent and public concerns. Encourages parental involvement.
Program Development	Responds to identified building needs. Provides growth opportunities for staff. Shares research with staff. Presents and/or publishes in education. Addresses state directives promptly. Provides for technologic growth.

would be documented by evidence that all teachers have been trained to use the system, that computers are now in every classroom, and that teachers meet weekly to discuss ways to integrate computer use into the curriculum and their classroom management activities.

Mentoring is an important allied resource for new administrators being supervised by a trait system. Mentors help to define the traits. Just as teachers must learn to work with a given curriculum and to address state and district objectives, so must an administrator learn how to function within each school system's political hierarchy and to adapt to that system's trait interpretations. Every system has a unique history that shapes its culture, a distinctly different way of conducting administrative business and looking at performance, and a chain of command and procedure—sometimes acknowledged in writing, sometimes not. Experienced administrators serving as mentors to the new and administratively challenged can play a significant role in helping administrators to "learn the ropes" before they find themselves dangling from them.

Group mentoring can also be an important source of assistance to a principal. Principals need the opportunity to talk to other principals in regularly set gatherings and to compare notes on all aspects of the job. Regular meetings with principals in and out of the district broaden the principal's perspective of the job and help the administrator to get a handle on the even bigger picture outside of district borders to which principal and district must respond.

Job Targets for Administrators

Once the Trait Model has identified areas of performance needing improvement, the supervisory approach can change to one of setting specific job targets for the principal. This method is akin to a combination of the Instructional Objectives and Performance Objectives Models discussed for teachers. A principal's classroom is the school, and instructional job targets can be defined by teacher, student, parent, or staff performance under the tutelage of a given principal. On the other hand, job targets addressing the principal's own performance will equate with performance objectives set for teachers addressing their work outside of the classroom. As with teachers, job targets for principals can be either remedial or progressive (i.e., they can be directed at helping principals who are not performing up to expectations to improve or they can be opportunities for exemplary principals to grow beyond expectations).

Job targets for principals, as with instructional objectives and performance objectives for teachers, should be objective, observable, and measurable. Principals have complained about a lack of clear expectations.[9] Thus, each target should be written with four distinct parts: *target, conditions, anticipated performance,* and *data indicating target achievement.*

1. The *target* should be described as a specific performance objective. For example, in the opening scenario, one of Taylor's targets might be to develop a school-wide discipline plan and to apply it consistently.
2. The *conditions* leading to the development of the discipline plan might include meeting with a committee of teachers during the weeks preceding the next scheduled faculty meeting to discuss discipline problems and ways to resolve these problems.
3. The *anticipated performance* would be the presentation and explication of the new discipline plan developed by the principal, working in collaboration with this faculty committee at the next scheduled faculty meeting.
4. The *data indicating target achievement* would be discipline referrals showing consistent implementation of the adopted school-wide discipline plan.

It is vital that job targets be as specific for principals as performance objectives are for teachers. Jobs are at stake, and specificity serves three purposes:

1. Targets that are specific give supervisory assistance because the principal knows what's expected.
2. Targets that are specific are objective.
3. Targets that are specific make it relatively easy to judge the level of target achievement.

Taylor, in the opening scenario, would need several job targets to bring performance up to expectations. When this happened with respect to a teacher's classroom performance, the supervisor prioritized instructional and/or performance objectives. However, it is difficult to prioritize job targets for principals. All aspects of a principal's job are important, and it is usually presumed that a principal is capable of addressing more than one job target at a time. In Taylor's case, other job targets would be required to address student performance and parent concern for safety. However, a consistent approach to discipline will affect both of these concerns. If discipline problems are controlled, teachers will be able to teach, students will be able to learn, and the chaotic environment accompanying poor and inconsistent disciplinary policies and safety concerns will be dispelled. Few job targets for principals can stand alone. One facet of the job inevitably has an impact on others.

Portfolio Supervision for Administrators

Another approach to principal supervision is an administrative portfolio appraisal system focusing on a purposeful, self-selected collection of artifacts and reflective entries that represent an administrator's growth.[10] In contrast to the requirements of the principal's Trait or Job Target Model, the principal self-supervises in creating a portfolio, including performance artifacts that reflect the principal's own documentation of professional and personal growth. Objective evidence is used, rather than subjective opinion (i.e., challenging curricula; student performance on competitive scales; innovative extracurricular programs; innovative staff development efforts; parent, teacher, and student surveys; grant funding; and evidence of local, state, and national status and reputation). The principal's own updated resume is the cornerstone for the portfolio—an outline summarizing growth for the school year.

As a professional with a career plan, portfolio self-assessment should be an annual routine for all administrators. The portfolio also identifies areas in need of attention in the coming year, projects not yet complete, or new interests and concerns. One cannot plan for where one wants to be without an understanding of where one has been.

The Charlotte-Mecklenburg System for Supervising Principals

The Charlotte-Mecklenburg Public School System has developed a system[11] for supervising its principals that uses a form of all three of the approaches discussed, with some interesting twists of its own. Principals report directly and often to the superintendent for guidance and direction.[12] The Charlotte-Mecklenburg System (CMS) measures a principal's effectiveness by looking at the extent to which:

1. academic benchmark goals are achieved;
2. patrons and clients are satisfied;
3. optimal conditions for learning are created; and
4. standards of responsible and ethical administrative practice are met.[13]

Principals receive points based on data on academic outcomes and the results of teacher, parent, and student surveys regarding the principal's performance.

Benchmark goals differ from school to school, depending on where a school stands academically. All principals have the opportunity to earn high ratings, based on a show of significant improvement from whatever academic starting point has been recorded. Thus, principals assigned to low-performing schools are encouraged to work for significant improvement. More importantly, all principals are required to acknowledge the role of employee and client satisfaction in overall performance ratings. Teachers, parents, and students become recognized supervisors in the CMS process.

The questions asked on teacher, parent, and student surveys are a form of Trait Model supervision, in that they highlight areas of performance concern. Parents are asked about school discipline and climate, communications and opportunities for involvement, as well as effective instruction and school administration. Teachers are asked to respond to questions about discipline and student behavior, management of school resources, open and supportive leadership, instructional leadership, student outcomes, and staff morale. Student perceptions on some of these same issues are sought through questions about discipline and student behavior, effective instruction, and communication and involvement from the student's perspective, but students are also asked about the school's climate and their perception of the school's expectations for them.[14]

Under the CMS system, each principal receives a thick, personalized notebook, complete with analyses of data on student achievement and the results of client surveys that inform, diagnose, and prescribe goals for the next supervision cycle. Essentially, the district creates for the principal a personalized portfolio to be used in the supervisory process.

CMS has also added an incentive and disincentive element to its supervision plan. Principals who earn a better-than-average overall rating under this system receive merit salary hikes of up to 10 percent, in addition to a school bonus awarded to all staff in achieving schools.[15] Principals who fail to make the grade are given one year to improve or face reassignment. Plans for improvement are developed directly under the supervision of the superintendent and target areas of specific weaknesses.

ADMINISTRATIVE SUPERVISION: A LEGAL PERSPECTIVE

In most states with collective bargaining laws, administrators are not part of the teacher unit. The separation recognizes an obvious conflict of interest between the roles of supervisors and administrators. Supervisory employees are not included in the bargaining unit because they exercise independent judgment and can discipline the employees that they supervise. To have both groups in the same collective bargaining unit would amount to having the "fox guarding the hen house." However, in many states, this same logic has left administrators with no collectively bargained rights.[16]

Administrators who are not covered by a district's collectively bargained agreement, however, still do retain all federal and state rights accorded them as citizens and employees. It can be argued that their discretionary status makes them virtually employees serving solely at the will of the hiring board. Nevertheless, boards of education and the superintendents acting as their agents cannot ignore an administrator's right to equal protection and due process. Administrators in danger of discipline or job loss can be expected to claim the same discrimination or liberty interests that a threatened teacher would claim. This does not mean that boards are powerless to remove administrators who perform below board expectations; it merely means that they, through the superintendent, must do their homework. The courts will uphold a board's decision to discipline or fire an administrator if the board can prove by a preponderance of evidence that, even if had not taken a discriminatory factor into account in making its decision, it would have acted in the same way, based on the administrator's performance record.[17] Boards and superintendents hoping to avoid having to defend employment decisions in court should take data collection and documented supervision seriously when dealing with administrators. The stakes are considerably higher than those for teachers, and it is unlikely that a disciplined or fired administrator will simply walk away with no future job prospects in sight.

THEORY INTO PRACTICE ACTIVITIES

1. Describe the administrators in your building, and what are their professional backgrounds (i.e., prior job experience).
2. Are the adminstrators in your building part of a collective bargaining unit?
3. If the administrators in your building do not collectively bargain, how are their contracts determined?
4. Do the administrators in your building have specific job descriptions?
5. Review the job descriptions for your building's administrators and discuss how these differ from teacher job descriptions.
6. Who supervises the administrators in your building, and what process is used?
7. Describe the procedures that must be followed in your district in order to discipline or dismiss an administrator.
8. What credentials are required in your district for appointment as an administrator?
9. What support groups exist to mentor new administrators in your district?
10. Who evaluates administrators in your district? Review the forms that are used.

NOTES

1. A.J. Reiman and L. Thies-Sprinthall, *Mentoring and Supervision for Teacher Development* (New York: Addison-Wesley Longman, 1998), 231.
2. E.J. Haller et al., "Does Graduate Training in Educational Administration Improve America's Schools?" *Phi Delta Kappan* 79, no. 3 (1997): 224.
3. G.B. Redfern, *How to Evaluate Teaching: A Performance Objectives Approach* (Worthington, OH: School Management Institute, 1972), 106.
4. R.A. Lindahl, "Evaluating the Principal's Performance: An Essential Step in Promoting School Excellence," *Education* 2 (1987): 204–241.
5. Redfern, *How to Evaluate Teaching: A Performance Objectives Approach,* 102.
6. Redfern, *How to Evaluate Teaching: A Performance Objectives Approach,* 102.

7. B.S. Portin et al., "The Changing Principalship and Its Impact: Voices from Principals," *National Association of Secondary School Principals Bulletin 82*, no. 602 (1998): 6.

8. Redfern, *How to Evaluate Teaching: A Performance Objectives Approach*, 103.

9. K.A. Leithwood, "Using the Principal Profile To Assess Performance," *Educational Leadership 1* (1987): 63–66.

10. G. Brown et al., "Taking the Lead: One District's Approach to Principal Evaluation," *National Association of Secondary School Principals 82*, no. 602 (1998): 19–20.

11. J.A. Murphy and S. Pimentel, "Grading Principals: Administrator Evaluations Come of Age," *Phi Delta Kappan 78*, no. 1 (1996): 74–81.

12. Murphy and Pimentel, "Grading Principals: Administrator Evaluations Come of Age," 75.

13. Murphy and Pimentel, "Grading Principals: Administrator Evaluations Come of Age," 75.

14. Murphy and Pimentel, "Grading Principals: Administrator Evaluations Come of Age," 78–79.

15. Murphy and Pimental, "Grading Principals: Administrator Evaluations Come of Age," 80.

16. See, e.g., *Ohio Revised Code* § 4117.01(F).

17. Price Waterhouse v. Hopkins, 490 U.S. 228 (1989).

15

Supervising Noncertified Employees

Supervising Noncertified Employees

The principal's secretary frequently discusses the letters she writes while lunching with other members of the secretarial pool. The head custodian is slow and surly in responding to teacher requests. The cafeteria supervisor insists on serving high-fat, low-nutrition lunches that satisfy students but cause parents to complain. The teaching assistants are absent more than present. The attendance clerk is rude to parents reporting student absences. The school bus driver ignores the district's prohibition against student smoking on the bus. The parking lot guard was found sleeping after a morning of drinking.

T he concept of differentiated supervision should not be limited to the supervision of teachers and certified employees. Schools employ many nonteaching, uncertified professionals and paraprofessionals who perform important functions and also need supervision. These nonteaching, uncertified employees include teachers' assistants, secretaries, cafeteria workers, custodians, bus drivers, and sundry other positions. All play a part in the successful functioning of a school, and all need a professional accountability plan and accompanying supervision. This chapter will explore ways to create meaningful professional accountability plans that will provide an outline for supervision for this wide range of employees.

There is no position in a school district that should go unsupervised. To assume that there is may result in costly consequences to both individuals and programs. Prospective administrators must have a clear understanding of what every paid employee in a school does if they are to supervise a cohesive educational program effectively. All roles are integral to the success of a school. A surly bus driver, a rude secretary, and an incompetent custodian will each play a part in undermining a school's mission. All are role models and resources for the students they are paid to serve. Each has a contracted role in the mission of the school. Therefore, these noncertified employees, not just teachers, must be put on notice concerning role expectations, and they must be supervised in their respective roles.

THE JOB DESCRIPTION

Most administrators come from the teaching ranks and have paid little or no attention to the cadre of support personnel needed to make a school function. Thus, one of the first jobs of any new administrator is to become familiar with each employee group within a building. It is important to know which groups have collectively bargained agreements and which positions are nonunionized. Collectively bargained contracts will usually play a significant role in defining how the employees they protect can be supervised, evaluated, rewarded, and disciplined. However, employees not covered by collectively bargained agreements will still retain their constitutional and federal rights regarding discrimination, notice, and due process.

Job descriptions are the starting point for every successful supervision plan. They satisfy the initial legal requirement for notice that is central to both employment and labor law. Just as for teachers and administrators, noncertified employees must also have a clear idea of the employer's expectations in order to be held accountable for performance. Thus, it remains essential to delineate the responsibilities for each position within a school and to let each employee know how performance will be monitored (i.e., what data will be gathered to show that areas of responsibility have been adequately addressed). Job descriptions for noncertified staff should also designate a supervisor—the person in charge of determining whether the employee is fulfilling the responsibilities assigned and complying with contract and work rules.

With this in mind, job descriptions for several noncertified positions have been developed in Appendix 15A, with a description of relevant data that can be used to monitor performance and a likely supervisor for the position. The job descriptions, relevant data, and named supervisors in these examples are not definitive, but these examples can be a catalyst, a beginning for a district's own efforts to define and assign responsibility to noncertified employees.

THE IMPORTANCE OF CONTRACT AND CONSISTENCY

Collectively bargained agreements, when they exist, will usually determine how noncertified staff in a given category will be evaluated, rewarded, and disciplined. Supervision, however, is not evaluation. Supervision for noncertified employees, like that for teachers, is assistance to do the task at hand as well as possible. The named supervisor for each position should provide the guidance and resources that an employee may need to fulfill the requirements of the job description.

Consistency is a vital part of successfully supervising noncertified employees. Employees within a given job classification have the right to know what to expect from those to whom they are responsible and to assume that all employees similarly situated will be treated in the same way. Consistent treatment is a central element of fairness, as is the proposition that no employee is beyond supervision. Most employees actually welcome fair and consistent supervision. Consistency means that there are clear job descriptions and guidelines for each position and that all employees within a given category will be supervised and, ultimately, evaluated with respect to that job description. The supervision plans may vary according to differentiated job descriptions, but there will be a plan for every employee, backed by data collected and analyzed by both the supervisor and the nonteaching employee.

Administrators who provide supervision for some but not all employees will seldom succeed in leading successful schools because, in the end, they will not be able to discipline any recalcitrant performer successfully. One of the ways that employees who are supervised and disagree with the form or degree of supervision will defend themselves is to charge that the supervisor is engaged in a campaign of personal harassment or liberty infringement. The unhappy employee will claim to have been singled out and treated differently from other employees.

Administrators, too, have job descriptions, and their own inconsistent compliance with those job descriptions can and will be used against them. The best defense is always a good offense, and administrators who do not provide supervision for all employees will find their failure to do so difficult to justify and impossible to refute.

Grievances and lawsuits are lost when disciplined employees can show inconsistent application of contract and supervision practice. Good school administrators do not pick and choose those who will be supervised. They are hired to supervise all employees within a school, either directly or indirectly through an administrative agent. If they don't, they will find it difficult or impossible to act when they must. Those employees supervised ad hoc will feel threatened, and those unsupervised will feel neglected. In both cases, the administrator or agent loses the ability to lead and to institute reform where needed. A case can be made that administrators who do not consistently supervise are illegally discriminating. Ultimately, there is a definite lack of respect, as well as legal protection for administrators who either cannot or will not do the job for which they have been hired.

THEORY INTO PRACTICE: ACTIVITIES

1. Develop a Job Description/Data Form for a school crossing guard.
2. Show the Job Description/Data Form in Activity 1 to a crossing guard and discuss its validity.
3. Should these forms be developed with the help of someone holding the position in question?
4. Develop a Job Description/Data Form for a school safety officer.
5. Review the form in Activity 4 with the building principal and discuss its validity.
6. Administrators should be aware of lines of responsibility and authority. Who is responsible for supervising the custodians in your school?
7. What role, if any, does the principal play in supervising the custodial staff?
8. Determine who is responsible for supervising other nonteaching support staff in your building.
9. What role, if any, does the principal play in supervising each of the positions discussed in this chapter?
10. Interview your building principal regarding any problems that might have been encountered in supervising nonteaching support staff.

Job Descriptions

Exhibit 15A–1 The Principal's Secretary (Supervisor: Principal)

Job Description Responsibility	Data Indicating Performance
Answer phones promptly and courteously.	Complaints by Those Calling
Accurately prepare all written communication.	Error-Free, Timely Communications
Keep an accurate appointment calendar.	Complaints or errors in Calendar
Maintain office confidentiality.	Documented Failure To Do So
Greet all promptly and courteously.	Documented Complaints or Observations
Keep records of all office activity.	Updated Files and Reports
Maintain a clean and efficient office.	Observed Office Appearance and Productivity Record
Update skills as required.	Evidence of Course Work/Training
Adapt to changing situations.	Examples of Willingness To Respond to Job Demands

Exhibit 15A–2 The Head Custodian (Supervisor: Assistant Principal)

Job Description Responsibility	Data Indicating Performance
Keep building clean.	Complaints and Specific Observations
Make all needed repairs promptly.	Complaints and Specific Observations
Give timely attention to work orders.	Complaints and Time Monitoring
Supervise custodial staff effectively.	Grievances and Complaints
File all requested reports.	File Copies and Complaints
Comply with all regulatory mandates.	Reports, Observations, and Official Violations
Provide inservice to staff as needed.	Record of Inservice Programs
Address all staff concerns.	Grievance Records
Evaluate staff as prescribed by contract.	Evaluation and Supervision Records

Exhibit 15A–3 The Teaching Assistant (Supervisor: Teacher)

Job Description Responsibility	Data Indicating Performance
Maintain regular attendance.	Attendance Record
Maintain good rapport with students.	Complaints and Observations
Follow directions.	Supervisor Observation and Documentation
Complete all assignments.	Supervisor Observation and Documentation
Adapt to changing situations.	Supervisor Observation and Documentation
Accept criticism.	Supervisor Observation and Documentation
Comply with administrative directives.	Supervisor Observation and Documentation
Support classroom teacher.	Teacher Observation and Documentation
Continue to learn.	Documented Course Work and Training

Exhibit 15A–4 The Cafeteria Supervisor (Supervisor: Principal)

Job Description Responsibility	Data Indicating Performance
Maintain inventory.	Record of Inventory
Comply with all government regulations.	Complaints and Official Violations
Prepare nutritious lunches.	Observations and Complaints
Adjust menus as requested.	Observations and Complaints
Maintain a clean work environment.	Observations and Official Violations
Relate well to staff.	Grievances and Complaints
Provide inservice to staff as needed.	Inservice Program Records
Supervise staff.	Evaluations and Supervision Records
Monitor program needs.	Observations and Complaints

Exhibit 15A–5 The Attendance Clerk (Supervisor: Assistant Principal)

Job Description Responsibility	Data Indicating Performance
Maintain regular attendance.	Attendance Record
Keep good records.	Complaints and Evidence of Error
Communicate with parents.	Record of Communications
Promptly report problems.	Records of Compliance and Complaints
Be courteous and helpful.	Complaints and Commendations
Follow administrative directives.	Administrator Observation
Solve attendance problems at lowest level.	Attendance Records
Relate positively to staff.	Record of Complaints and Commendations
Work to improve data collection.	Record of Procedures and Innovations

Exhibit 15A–6 The School Bus Driver (Supervisor: Assistant Principal)

Job Description Responsibility	Data Indicating Performance
Report regularly for bus duty.	Attendance Record
Follow directions.	Record of Pick-Up and Delivery
Follow driving laws.	Citations and Fines
Comply with safety procedures.	Routine Inspections
Maintain time schedule.	Record of Arrivals
Maintain prescribed discipline on bus.	Referral Records
Drive safely.	Accident Record
Consult regularly with Administration.	Record of Meetings
Submit to regular physicals.	Physical Records

Exhibit 15A–7 The Parking Lot Guard (Supervisor: Assistant Principal)

Job Description Responsibility	Data Indicating Performance
Report for work regularly.	Attendance Record
Follow directions.	Complaints and Referrals
Protect cars and students.	Record of Interventions
Report unauthorized conduct.	Referrals
Remain alert at all times.	Observations and Complaints
Maintain good rapport with staff and students.	Record of Comments and Complaints
Follow all work rules.	Record of Complaints and Observations
Maintain order in the parking lot.	Record of Disturbances in the Parking Lot
Report suspected criminal activity to police.	Relevant Police Reports

Afterword

Supervision of the school program is not a monolithic process. Schools operate successfully through the efforts of a wide range of individuals, each playing a unique and important role in the educational process. It is foolish to assume that any one form or process can be used to supervise every employee in the school community effectively. Jobs differ and people differ, even within employment groups and collective bargaining units. Thus, efforts to clarify job expectations and to help school employees fulfill those expectations demand differentiation.

Supervision is not evaluation. Supervision is not an effort to assess employee performance, but rather an effort to assist individual employees in defining and developing their roles within the school community so that they contribute to the effectiveness of the overall educational program.

This text has tried to stress the importance of remediation, both legally and practically, in helping administrators, teachers, nonteaching certified employees, and noncertified support personnel to achieve optimum performance. Thoughtful, differentiated supervision is the key to attaining and maintaining an effective educational program.

Table of Cases

Index

Page numbers in *italics* denote figures and exhibits.

257